# FAMILY THERAPY

## FOR EVERYONE

# *How to get the best out of living together*

### Dr Eia Asen

BBC BOOKS

# Acknowledgements

Much of what is in this book I have learned from over a thousand families and couples I have treated over the past two decades. And many of the ideas are based on the work of the great pioneers of family therapy, including Bateson, Jackson, Palazzoli, Minuchin, Haley, Watzlawick, Satir, Whitaker, and others too numerous to mention.

I have learned a great deal from my family therapy teachers and friends and I feel particularly indebted to Luigi Boscolo, Gianfranco Cecchin, Alan Cooklin, Gill Gorrell-Barnes, Judy Hildebrand, Elsa Jones, Peter Lomas, Ann Miller, Salvador Minuchin, Heiner Schuff, Ann Stevens, Peter Tomson, Arthuro Varchevker and Carl Whitaker.

As far as this book is concerned I have had plenty of help from a number of people who have tried to steer me away from the psychiatrist's often warped perceptions of ordinary family life. I would like to thank Sheila Ableman and Charlotte Lochhead of BBC Books on this count. If the book proves to be readable then much of the credit goes to the editor Kelly Davis who tried to knock some common sense into the manuscript. Minna Daume also helped to edit the manuscript at an earlier stage. Last but not least, I want to thank my wife Denise, who with her incisive mind and irreverent questioning not only helped me enormously to clarify my ideas, but also supported me throughout this whole project in such a way that no therapy was required for our own family.

This book is published to accompany the television series entitled
*Family Therapy* which was first broadcast in April, 1995
Executive Producer Udi Eichler
Producer and Director Peter Gordon

Published by BBC Books,
an imprint of BBC Worldwide Publishing, BBC Worldwide Ltd,
Woodlands, 80 Wood Lane, London, W12 0TT

First published 1995
© Dr Eia K Asen 1995
ISBN 0 563 37054 8

Designed by William Mason
Illustrations by Ian Dicks
Set in New Baskerville
Typesetting by Ace Filmsetting Ltd, Frome, Somerset
Printed and bound in Great Britain by Clays Ltd, St Ives plc
Cover printed by Clays Ltd, St Ives plc

# Contents

# Introduction

*Why do some families seem to be addicted to arguing? What attracts people to one another? How come we have the power to drive those close to us mad? How is it that a wife may prefer her husband when he is depressed rather than when he is feeling well? Why when I hated my mum did I end up with a wife just like her? What is it about those we love that makes us wish to move as far away as posible from them? When is it time to leave home? Do families need secrets? Is it possible to predict family crises? Who can help to sort out family problems?*

Family life is full of drama – from adolescent love affairs to marital screaming matches, from family feuds to old-age blues. We may act the 'happy family' to the outside world, but go for each other's throats the moment we are behind closed doors. Sometimes we involve others in our dramas: grandparents, uncles and aunts, cats and dogs, neighbours, lawyers and doctors – even the media!

*Family Therapy for Everyone* examines family life from birth to death, describes many familiar scenarios and gives practical advice on how to step out of uncomfortable roles. It also suggests how to write new endings to old 'scripts' that have been passed on to us by our elders. *Family Therapy for Everyone* challenges the notion that we are the victims of our own fate and suggests some 'Do It Yourself' exercises aimed at spotting problems and starting to resolve them. The book encourages families to help themselves. The ideas put forward are meant to act as catalysts rather than specific solutions. It's impossible to provide solutions that will work for everyone because we all come from different cultures, with different experiences and unique family backgrounds.

The book also contains many descriptions of case histories. Based on real families, they are meant to illustrate common relationship issues. Every effort has been made to change the names of the families and individuals concerned and to alter other identifiable details. Many case histories are deliberately not concluded because they only apply to specific people.

Different outcomes are possible, depending on the characteristics of the particular family. I do not want to give the impression in this book that there are simple prescriptions for problems which are often very complex.

*Family Therapy for Everyone* aims to:

– provide an insight into how families work
– get you to look at your own and other families from a different perspective
– help you identify and address problematic areas of family life
– enable you to untie relationship knots
– help you have better relationships inside and outside your family.

*Family Therapy for Everyone* is meant to be fun but also to shed some new light on family life. Nobody should feel compelled to do any of the DIY exercises, particularly if change is the last thing you or your family require. You may decide not to try some of the exercises because you think they might be too upsetting. If you do have a go, take care. This book is not a substitute for therapy, and professional help is sometimes essential. The last chapter describes what family therapy is all about and how to go about finding appropriate help, if you feel you need it. You may also wish to consult the Further Reading and Useful Addresses sections for more information on some of the problems touched on in this book.

## Chapter 1

# What is a family?

IN THIS CHAPTER WE LOOK AT:
•
WHAT FAMILIES MEAN TO US
•
HOW FAMILIES ARE STRUCTURED
•
FAMILY TREES
•
FAMILY SECRETS

## WHAT DO FAMILIES MEAN TO US?

Different cultures have very different notions of what constitutes a family. Whereas monogamy is the rule in most Western societies, there are some countries where it is quite acceptable for men to have several wives. Likewise, in different historical periods people have seen the family in very different ways. In Britain a few hundred years ago, for example, the family included everyone who lived under one roof – parents, children, grandparents and servants.

Nowadays the word 'family' is used as if it had one universal meaning. To many it conjures up an image of two parents of opposite sexes and two children living in domestic bliss, perhaps with some doting grandparents down the road. Such families are thought of as 'normal', though for most people the reality is quite different. These days there are all sorts of

families, including unmarried couples, single parents, recon-
stituted families, childless couples, communes, and lesbian
and gay couples with children.

In this book the word 'family' refers to any group of people
who are committed to nurture one another emotionally and
physically. In this sense the family can include members of the
extended family, close friends and partners.

### WHO NEEDS FAMILIES?

Some people think they can break away from their families,
perhaps by living in another country. But the truth is that
families are inescapable. Even when there is an ocean between
us and our not-so-loved ones we carry them in our heads.
Nothing and nobody can evoke feelings as strong, and sometimes as destructive, as our families. If you doubt this, consider
the story of Kate.

*Kate was nineteen when she left her native England and
emigrated to Australia – to get away from her parents with
whom she'd always had a difficult relationship. When she left,
her parents were hurt and told their friends that she was 'no
longer part of the family'.*

*Despite the enormous distance between herself and those she
once loved, Kate found herself thinking about them more and
more every day. The more she thought about them the angrier
she became. Some days she felt such hatred for her mother that
she could not bring herself to eat anything. Kate became
seriously anorexic and lost 4 stone. She had to be admitted to
hospital. At that point her parents flew out to Australia.*

*When physically recovered, Kate returned with her parents to
her home in England. Here they lived through months of
confrontations – initially only over food, but then increasingly
over other issues. With some outside professional help, Kate was
able to negotiate her own space in the family. When she moved
out into a flat around the corner some ten months later she felt
more independent than she had been in Australia. She was able
to think about matters other than her family whom she went to*

*see once a week – for Sunday lunch. She said: 'I now feel that there is more real distance between myself and my family than when we lived 10 000 miles apart.'*

## THE FAMILY AS AN ORGANIZATION

When we meet new people accompanied by partners, parents or children, we are likely to refer to them as a family. We might describe them afterwards as 'a really nice family' or 'a dreadful family'. Even though we may know the family members as individuals, with their own specific characteristics, we still tend to give them some sort of family 'identity'.

No family is identical. Like any organization, each family has its own specific characteristics and rules. Its fragile equilibrium can be upset by many different factors, such as illness, unemployment, or the addition or loss of a member. In the face of a crisis families try to discover ways of establishing a new balance.

If the father is ill, another family member may have to take over certain jobs temporarily. With their first baby born, parents need to make a major readjustment in their lifestyle. If a family cannot cope with such a transition then one or more members may develop problems. Such problems, whilst they may appear to concern only one person, are usually connected with the way family members relate to one another. What the mother does affects her son, whose response in turn affects his sister, who cannot help but affect her father. Thus a chain reaction is set in motion.

Family organization changes over time to adapt to external and internal pressures. When there is a major threat from outside, a family will generally show a united front, sometimes with positive results as in the case of Paul.

*When Paul, the Smiths' teenage son, first got into trouble at school, his parents were up in arms and complained to the head teacher. Even though Paul had been no angel at home for some time, the whole family claimed that Paul would never misbehave and acted as if they had all been attacked by a common enemy. Paul was visibly pleased by this show of family loyalty and his performance at school started to improve. His parents, encouraged by the change, then helped him with his unruly behaviour at home.*

## WHO'S TELLING THE TRUTH?

As we have seen, families are made up of individuals and we each have our own point of view or version of the truth. If we could all see other points of view, family life would be a lot more peaceful. Unfortunately, when we are locked in an argument, the only point of view we can see is our own. Consider the following:

Question: Who started it?
  A: *'You did.'*
  B: *'No, you did.'*
  A: *'No, you did.'*

---

DIY EXERCISE: TAKING A BIRD'S EYE VIEW

---

- Try to remember the last unpleasant exchange you had with someone near and dear to you. Picture what took place.
- Now imagine that you have floated up to the furthest corner of the ceiling (or the sky if it took place outside).
- View the same scene from above – taking a bird's eye view. You see two (or more) people interacting, one of whom is you.
- Does it look different? Can you see the part you play? Observe the body language, listen to the tone of voice. Do you just react to the other person – or do you provoke them a bit?
- See whether you can connect the words and actions of one person with those of the other(s).
- Practise this a few times, remembering different exchanges. Then, next time you are in the thick of some family drama, try taking a bird's eye view and see whether it changes the situation.

B: *'I didn't.'*
A: *'Yes, you did.'*

Does it matter who started it?

Sometimes, in the case of wars or other man-made disasters, it is important to establish who started it all. Yet even observers and historians usually disagree on the causes of such events.

Family historians are no more reliable. It is all a question of observer bias. 'I drink because he upsets me' is one version of the truth. There is at least one other possible version: 'I am only upset because she drinks.'

It is often difficult for the people involved in such an argument to see each other's perspective, so it may require an outsider to point out the circularity of the situation. Her drinking may be a response to him upsetting her, which in itself is a response to her drinking, which in turn is triggered by him upsetting her, and so on. If the couple can take a few steps back and recognize that they are both caught in a trap, they can stop feeling the need to blame each other. Then they can start considering ways of solving the underlying problem together.

In the heat of an argument it is not easy to detach oneself sufficiently to see things from a different perspective, but it's always worth trying. The following exercise offers one method of distancing yourself from such a situation in order to gain a more balanced view of what's really going on.

### IDENTIFYING THE FAMILY STRUCTURE

Standing back, or seeing things from a different perspective, enables us to identify the patterns of behaviour that exist in most families. These patterns might, for example, include:

– constant arguments between a mother and her teenage daughter
– the father distancing himself from the family when there are tears
– alliances between the grandmother and the child against a parent
– frequent bickering between two partners about household chores

Taken together, such patterns form the structure of the family – the expected ways of behaving and relating to each other. Like a historic building, the family structure may have been stable for years, but – because it's finely balanced – it can still be fragile. As in an old building, individual members have stress points which can cause them, or the family, to collapse under pressure.

For all these reasons it's important to understand the structure of the family and identify the stress points which need to be strengthened. To do this, we can draw a family relationship map, illustrating the relationships between different family members. By using various symbols for closeness, distance, love, mixed feelings, etc, the map can show who has the power in the family, who supports that person and who doesn't, where the major conflicts are, and who is close to whom.

The first diagram shows how an outside observer perceives the Jones family, consisting of Mother, maternal Grandmother ('Nan'), Father, Jack (15) and Jill (8). This map reveals a very

**Outsider's view of family**

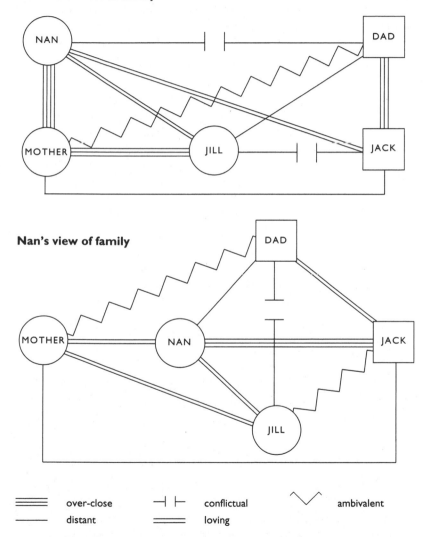

**Nan's view of family**

Hierarchies in the family are signified by who is at the top and who is at the bottom of the map

close relationship between all the women, with the men hovering on the periphery of family life.

However it is important to remember that such maps are highly subjective snapshots. The same person might draw a totally different diagram at a different time – for instance when he or she is intensely angry with a certain member of the family. Moreover, other members of the family would probably come up with quite different maps of the same family, depending on their individual bias. Nan, for example, drew the second map on page 13, showing a very close relationship between her and her grandson.

Clearly, the way we see things has a lot to do with our position in the family. And at different times we may have quite different perceptions of ourselves and others, depending on our current loves or hates.

---

DIY EXERCISE: PUT YOUR FAMILY ON THE MAP

Take some time over this exercise.
• Draw your own relationship map on a piece of paper.
• Put yourself in the middle and then place members of your immediate and extended family, friends or partners around you.
• Use symbols to describe the various relationships between members of your family.
• To illustrate the shifting nature of such snapshots, you might consider how you would have drawn this map a year ago – or perhaps prior to some major change in your immediate or wider family (such as illness, leaving home or changing job).
• Now draw your ideal map of family relations – how you would like things to be, say in a year's time.
• Think about what would have to change to achieve this. Talk about it with your partner, parent or child – but avoid hurting one another!
• Ask another family member to draw his or her family map – and then discuss the similarities and differences.

## Who is who in the family?

Family maps contain information on current family relationships, but say little about how they have been formed. Constructing a family tree is a way of putting the entire cast on the map. This makes it possible to have a closer look at the various people involved in the family drama and the roles they play.

Here then is a two-generational family tree:

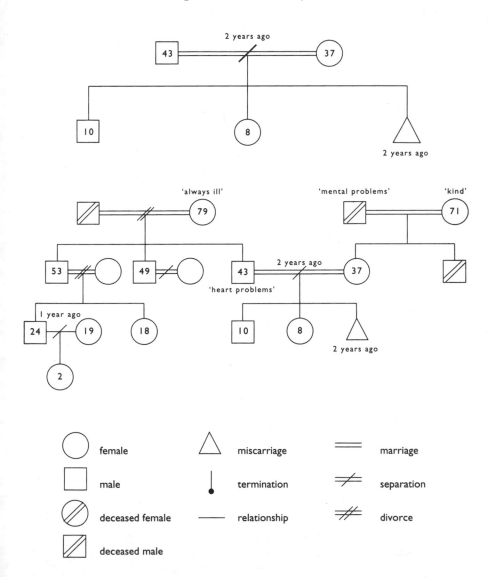

The first family tree is of a one-parent family – two children living with their mother. The parents separated, around the time of a miscarriage. To annotate family trees in shorthand, specific symbols can be used like those in the key on page 15.

If we include previous generations of this family the tree looks like the second diagram. On Father's side we have a pattern of divorce and separation. On Mother's side a lot of people seem to die young. It is possible to record any information on a family tree diagram – names, personal characteristics, dates of birth and death. It is even possible to superimpose a relationship map onto this to show who was closest to whom and where the major conflicts existed.

There is no limit to the type and number of questions you might wish to ask – many others will be raised in the next few chapters. Often, when investigating a family tree, one comes across areas of uncertainty or total lack of knowledge. The first thing to ask yourself is why don't you know? Secondly, who would know the answer to that question? This may tempt you to talk to that person.

When looking at your partner's family tree, you might try to spot similarities and differences between your two families. You could look out for similarities in background, profession, religion, place of origin, size of family, etc. There is no need to restrain your curiosity. The more people you involve in discussing the tree, the more interesting and revealing the results.

But a word of warning: exploring one's family tree can be upsetting. Old wounds can get reopened, bad memories revived and blame apportioned. However, discussing relationships by looking at a family tree allows you to view your family affairs from a different perspective, and that's nearly always a good thing.

## FAMILY BELIEFS AND MYTHS

Once you've worked out your family tree, you can explore family myths and secrets. All families have their own belief systems, about what is good or bad, what's on and what's not on. Some of these beliefs arc openly stated; others are implicit

DIY EXERCISE: DRAW YOUR OWN FAMILY TREE

This is another exercise that can be upsetting to some.
- On a large piece of paper put yourself in first – circle for female, square for male.
- If you have a partner, put him or her next to you. Then add any children or grandchildren you may have.
- Now go back a generation and put in your parents and your siblings. Put in your grandparents and any other relations.
- Inside each square or circle write the age and/or date of death. You can add the name, and any illnesses or problems.
- Write at least one word that comes to mind next to each name. It doesn't matter whether it is a problem, attribute or illness (e.g. 'unforgiving', 'kind', 'suicide' or 'cancer').
- If you've a partner do the same for his/her side of the tree.
- Fill it in as accurately as possible. Leave gaps or question marks if there are any bits of information you don't have.
- With a different coloured pen you could draw in the quality of the relationships: close, distant, coalitions, conflicts etc.
- Look at the tree. Can you see anything new about your family? Discuss it with a friend or family member. Consider how this tree might 'explain' some of the problems or preoccupations you have encountered in your present life.
- Now look at the tree and ask the following questions:
  - Who do you think you are most like?
  - Who do others think you are most like?
  - What is it about that person that makes others think you are like him/her?
  - Who has had a problem similar to yours?
  - Who has had problems similar to those of other members of your family?
  - Who is most/least supportive?
  - Look at any two people on the tree: What was their relationship like? Repeat this with any other pair.
  - From which of these people would you keep your problems secret? Why?
  - Who never talks about their problems? Why?
  - Who is the scapegoat in each generation?

and only become obvious when someone – knowingly or un-knowingly – breaks the rules. For instance, many families hold firm beliefs about what men or women are allegedly 'good at' – and 'not good at'. It takes considerable strength to stand up against such beliefs. When men whose families see them as 'practical' and 'good with their hands' behave as if they are unable to replace a fuse, and become poets or nannies instead, deeply embedded belief systems get challenged. Similarly, women who decide to embark on so-called 'male' careers, such as airline pilot, football coach or brain surgeon, often defy the belief systems of large sections of society as well as their imme-diate family.

Family beliefs can express themselves through stories or legends. Myths are distorted beliefs which people hold on to despite evidence that they are untrue. In some ways a myth functions like a thermostat that is switched on according to the temperature, thereby regulating and 'cooling down' family relationships. Myths come into play whenever family tension raises sufficiently to threaten relationships. An example is the myth that 'You simply cannot trust men.'

> *When Jane, in her early twenties and an only daughter, fell in love with Joe, her parents were desolate. She had been groomed to look after them and Joe's arrival on the scene was a threat to their long-term plans. This led to the revival of the potent family myth that 'You simply cannot trust men' and much evidence was supplied – some of it true, some distorted.*
>
> *This myth gradually poisoned Jane's relationship with Joe. She became increasingly reluctant to see him, particularly since she felt she had to be loyal to her father – who was held up as the notable exception that proved the rule. Joe, feeling rejected, eventually started an affair with another woman. When this came to light, nobody was surprised, since in this family everyone knew that 'You simply cannot trust men'.*

Most families invent their own stories or myths. The past is painted in a certain way so that a point about the present can be made. On the one hand myths are convenient, helping the family to avoid confronting some awful truth. On the other hand, they can become like blinkers, imposing a rigid view of past and present.

Here are a few rather common family myths:

– Women in our family always have problems.
– He is Dad's favourite child and that will never change.
– My parents' marriage was perfect. They never argued.
– Grandparents know best.
– We are a happy family. We are never sad.

*Paul and Bill, fourteen and sixteen, had been brought up by their uncle and aunt, having been told that their own parents were 'too crazy' to look after them. As they grew older they started to examine these so-called 'facts'. The more contact they had with their natural parents, the more they doubted their alleged craziness. When Paul and Bill discussed this with their uncle and aunt, they were told that if they couldn't see that their parents were mad, this would cast some doubt on their own sanity. Challenging this myth did not seem possible, and this blocked Paul and Bill's wish to have an independent relationship with their natural parents.*

*For a time they avoided seeing their natural parents. However when Paul and Bill reached their late teens they became curious again. They wondered whether they had perhaps inherited some of their parents' 'crazy' traits. Both made contact with their birth parents, who were by now separated and lived in different parts of the country. They got to know each of them and discovered some of the reasons why their birth parents had been unable to bring them up. Paul and Bill found out about long-standing family feuds, their mother's family's rejection of their father, the wish of their childless uncle and aunt to have children, and the young parents' own enormous relationship battles.*

*With hindsight, Paul and Bill were grateful that their uncle and aunt had not exposed them to all this information during their adolescence. They would have found it all rather confusing during an already difficult time – and their feelings might have proved too much for them. However a few years later the time seemed right to contact their birth parents and compare the myths with the reality. As adults, both Paul and Bill managed to have good relationships not only with their adoptive parents but also with their birth parents.*

## FAMILY SECRETS

Often family myths are created to hide shameful events or secrets. Almost all families have secrets. A secret is often some important information that is withheld because of fear that it might affect our relationships. Many a secret is not secret at all: everybody seems to know what 'it' is, but nobody dare mention 'it' openly. There is an unspoken agreement not to talk about 'it'. 'It' could be an entirely harmless secret or a dreadful dark secret – but without speaking about 'it' there is no way of finding out. In fact, many secrets are petty and it is not their actual content that is so disturbing, but the way people behave when trying to keep secrets.

Saying 'I know something that is secret' is a perfect wind-up, leading to all kinds of speculation and coalitions between different family members. Such teasing can be paralysing, keeping everyone guessing – as there is innuendo but no evidence. The most powerful secrets in families have to do with sex, violence, death and money.

Children have a remarkable ability to sense secrets. Their parents' tone of voice or facial expression may indicate that something is being hidden. If the parents *say* that there is no secret, but their body language and other non-verbal cues *show* there is, children can become confused. The result is a loss of trust.

Sometimes children invent their own stories to cope with this confusion and such stories may indicate their knowledge of what the secret is about. A child may invent an imaginary companion who has the name of a dead sibling – whom the parents never mention. Another child, from whom some dreadful family illness has been kept secret, may be excessively keen on games to do with hospitals. It is surprising how few parents make the obvious connection, perhaps because they themselves find it so hard to acknowledge the existence of the 'secret'.

**Why is it important to have secrets?**

People have quite different opinions as to whether or not to have and keep secrets. Benevolent secrets, for instance, may involve not telling children what they are getting for Christmas in order to give them the pleasure of a surprise present. Many parents believe that certain things should not be discussed with young children. These taboo subjects may include the parents' sexual relationship or financial problems, or the circumstances of a relative's death (for instance a suicide or a stillbirth). Other parents think it is absolutely wrong to keep anything secret from their offspring and will involve them from toddlerhood onwards in any and all family business.

Many people tend to differentiate between constructive and destructive secrets and between privacy and secrecy. Yet drawing the line is difficult. Where does privacy end and secrecy start? Secrecy comes into play when, for whatever reason, we want to protect others from some information. Very often we are secretive to avoid the effect on us of someone's response to knowing about the secret.

It is important to understand why a secret has come into being in the first place. There may have been good reasons for it at the time. The question is whether these reasons are still valid *now*. Further questions can then be asked:

– What are the advantages and disadvantages of the secret being revealed now?
– How can this best be done?
– Who should do the telling?

Tracking the history of a secret can be a hard job. When a member of the family plucks up enough courage to challenge an important secret, the whole family structure may resist or crumble. Secrets, even if created by one person, soon become the property of the family, which may itself have the power to weaken or strengthen the effect of those secrets.

Secrets may be known by only one family member – or openly or secretly shared with others, but not necessarily by everyone. Some secrets are known to everyone inside the immediate family but not to the outside world, usually because of some dreadful feared consequence, such as the involvement of police or feuds with the extended family. Some secrets involve only two people who swear one another to total secrecy, or one person intimidates another and threatens violence if the secret is revealed. One of the most common and least talked about dreadful family secrets is that of incest and particularly sexual abuse of a child by a parent. To the abuse survivor it feels like a 'lonely secret', impossible to share with anyone. The survivor may therefore hold on to it for decades – or forever.

Secrets can be useful for families but harmful at the same time. When nobody speaks about the unspeakable, powerful family myths can evolve, including the myth that 'We are a family without any secrets.' Secrets can destroy trust and closeness in the family.

*When Phil turned sixteen home life became increasingly unbearable. He felt 'different' but did not know why. His behaviour at home was often outrageous and his parents repeatedly told him 'If you go on like this you won't be one of us.' Tearing their hair out, they would exclaim that they had 'no idea where this is all coming from . . . we didn't teach you that'. The more they ran Phil down, the worse his behaviour got. He felt rejected and frequently said to his father: 'I wish you weren't my dad.'*

*Eventually the family reached crisis point. Phil's father lost control and burst out: 'You're just like your father!' This line opened a Pandora's Box: it turned out that Phil was the product of an incestuous relationship between his mother and her father – an extremely well-kept secret. When it had happened everyone had been sworn to secrecy and a respectable husband had been found for the young mother. Phil's 'different' outrageous behaviour had had the effect of blowing open the secret.*

## Secret fears

Most secrets are rooted in fact and some in fantasy. The latter have to do with anxieties based on feelings like love, hate, jealousy or rejection. Such fears can be shared by other members of the family, often without anything being said. People behave as if they were waiting for a terrible curse to come true and their excessive worrying may turn this fear into a self-fulfilling prophecy.

*Peter was twelve when his behaviour at school began to cause enormous concern. Teachers reported that he seemed to be hearing voices in his head and was visibly listening to them during lessons, making him unable to participate in classroom activities. He soon became the victim of considerable teasing by his fellow pupils.*

*When he and his parents saw a child psychiatrist at a clinic, his mother signalled with winks and other non-verbal clues that there was something she wanted to say when Peter was not present. She made an excuse for Peter to leave the room and prefaced her disclosure by stating that she had never told her husband – who was now present in the room – how worried she was that Peter might turn out to be 'a schizophrenic', just like her own father. She talked about the horrendous childhood she had endured, with her own father hearing voices and acting cruelly towards her.*

*When Peter was born she was struck by his physical similarity to his grandfather and she could not get the thought out of her head that he might become 'schizophrenic' too. Peter's mother then described how through his early childhood she watched him*

*closely to detect traits resembling those of his grandfather. She
kept her fears secret, petrified that they might come true if she
voiced them. Her husband listened to this account and then, to
his wife's surprise, confessed that he had had identical fears but
had never voiced them because he did not want to worry his
wife. When Peter was later invited back to the room he was
asked what he thought his mother had wanted to talk about
without him being present. Without any hesitation he replied,
'About my grandad. He was mad.'*

It seems to be a fairly universal truth that parents cannot help
worrying about their children. At times they detect a trait in a
child that reminds them of the past, evoking fears that are
often too awful to be talked about. Clearly, sitting on secrets
makes them worse and finding someone to share the secret
with is half the battle.

## Secret alliances

Secrets can become powerful weapons in daily family battles.
When only two people know, strong alliances may result, often
crossing the generations. If children are involved they soon
feel uncomfortable and tend to draw attention to secrets: they
may whisper something to the confidante in the presence of
the person from whom something is supposed to be kept
secret. This naturally arouses curiosity if not suspicion.

Often the very existence of a secret causes excitement, irrespective of what it is about. The mere act of secret-keeping is
all-important, making the one who is not in the know feel left
out. This can lead to tantalizing guessing games.

*Jane, thirteen, accidentally found out about her mother's affair
with a married man. Jane hinted that she knew something but
her mother ignored the hints until Jane eventually confronted
her and was sworn to secrecy. Jane felt the need to share the
secret and told her sister Kate, swearing her to secrecy. Kate in
turn told her maternal uncle who told his mother, also swearing
her to secrecy. Jane's father meanwhile knew that Jane had a
secret and asked his wife why Jane was acting so odd. Jane's
mother denied knowing why, but was sufficiently worried to*

---

DIY EXERCISE: SECRET BUSTING

---

Here are a few suggestions on how to deal with secrets:

1 **Identify the secret, name it.**

Most secrets have to do with sex, illness or death.

2 **Evaluate the pros and cons of secret-keeping.**

Ask the following questions:

– How does the secret affect family life? Who's stressed and how?

– How is open communication between family members affected by the secret? Who cannot talk to whom, when and with whom present?

– What would be the worst outcome if the secret was revealed? Who'd be most affected – and in what way?

– What would be the best outcome? Who'd be most helped?

– Who probably does know about the secret?

– Who could talk about the secret, to whom and when?

3 **Consider the risks of owning up:**

– shame

– loss of trust

– reaction among family members e.g. rage, hurt

– safety issues reprisals or threats.

4 **Consider the benefits of owning up:**

– relief

– possibility of mending and healing

– greater openness and subsequent trust

– increased honesty.

5 **Now decide when and where to bust the secret!**

---

*consult her own mother. She in turn had been told by her son (Kate and Jane's uncle) not to let on that she knew but her overacting was not very convincing and alerted her daughter to wonder what secret her mother had. She later asked Jane whether she had revealed her secret. Jane vehemently denied this.*

Secret-keeping can tie people up in knots. It is a minefield, and subtle and not-so-subtle forms of blackmail are another consequence. 'I won't tell anyone about your secret if you do this for me' is a not uncommon request.

*Chapter 2*

# Routines and survival techniques

IN THIS CHAPTER WE LOOK AT:

•

HOW ROUTINES DEVELOP IN FAMILIES

•

ARGUMENTS AND HOW THEY CAN BE STOPPED

•

ALLIANCES BETWEEN DIFFERENT FAMILY
MEMBERS

•

SCAPEGOATING

•

OVER-CLOSE AND DISTANT FAMILIES

•

HOW FAMILIES CAN DRIVE PEOPLE MAD

## WHY FAMILIES NEED ROUTINES

Much of family life is a routine affair. Family outings and gatherings – to celebrate anniversaries or religious festivals – are examples of routines with which everyone is familiar. On a smaller scale daily life is full of routines, many of which are comforting and reassuring. The bedtime story or early morning cup of tea are signals that all is well. Who lays the table and who does the washing up may be fixed and any deviation from this may seem odd. Doing the same old thing over and over again makes us feel at home.

Yet some set routines are less positive. Take, for instance, the one involving the husband who comes home from work, puts his feet up and expects his wife to serve him dinner in front of the television. He may like this routine but she probably gets increasingly tired of it. In other families we may observe that 'They always argue' or that 'He is never on her side'. These are all behaviour patterns which have become characteristic of certain families. They are what makes them tick. However some routines can have long-term damaging effects. For example, if a young person is repeatedly told that he is 'no good' then it is only a question of time before his behaviour is affected by this daily dose of poison.

We are not usually aware of most of these routines, particularly when they feel good. They just seem to happen automatically. In any case it is not always easy to distinguish between good and bad routines. Some routines seem bad for one family, yet fine for others. For example, some families routinely argue and believe that this is character-forming. The silence between arguments becomes unbearable, as if the only way they can show affection for one another is through heated arguments.

Other families are proud that they never argue. So, what may be a problem to one person or family could be 'normal' to another. To complicate matters further, some people in a family setting seem to be addicted to what hurts them. This isn't all that surprising: habits such as smoking and drinking are known to be harmful but that in no way diminishes the pleasure we get from them. There are those who become addicted to marital violence, to scapegoating others, or to putting themselves down, and they view this as normal.

In a reasonably average family what are the signals which suggest that all is not well? Let's look at specific ways of changing some common entrenched routines which can cause distress – outbursts, arguments, malignant alliances, scapegoating, loving people to death, putting people down and driving people mad.

## OUTBURSTS

It may seem strange to think of outbursts as routines because they appear to come out of the blue. Yet most outbursts follow a pattern which reflects underlying problems.

'You are silly!' How often have we heard this said about ourselves? Probably too often to be touched by it – except very occasionally. At those times, however, this little remark can make some of us erupt like a volcano. To those who find themselves near the fall-out zone the response often seems quite out of proportion to the provocation.

*Joe was known to everyone as a highly efficient man, not only at work but also in his home. His family saw him as a tower of strength and admired his independence. He went on many business trips and always returned in a cheerful mood. When at home he would also do his fair share of household chores. All seemed well.*

*From time to time, however, he went into crisis. This always seemed to coincide with his wife going away for a day or two to see her parents. Shortly before her departure Joe would be irritable and say that it wasn't fair that the children, now in*

*their late teens, were being left 'on their own'. He would
alternate between being very angry with his wife and behaving
as if he was very depressed. His wife Judy could make no sense
of this and, since Joe was unwilling to discuss the matter any
further, this routine went on for years.*

*When the oldest child left home Joe became very depressed.
After a lot of probing he was able to tell his wife how he had felt
abandoned by his mother when he was little. His mother's father
had been widowed and chronically ill which required her to
spend much time looking after him, resulting in long absences
from home. Joe had been badly affected by this and had 'coped'
by growing into premature independence. He had never made
the connection between his early experiences and the outbursts
during his married life, possibly because it was too painful to
remember his own sense of desertion. Every time his wife decided
to go and see her parents, he had 'seen red' and unconsciously
re-experienced his early abandonment.*

*Telling his wife Judy about how he felt deserted by his mother
was Joe's first step towards sharing his hurt and connecting the
present with the past. It also made him feel very vulnerable,
something he had been trying to hide behind his façade of
capable independence. Judy responded well to this change in
Joe's attitude, and they were able to have more open discussions
about a variety of sensitive issues. Joe gradually learned to
accept that his wife was very different from his mother. His
outbursts slowly disappeared.*

When circumstances in the present resemble those of the past,
old feelings can get re-evoked. Something in us resonates and
often we do not know what it is. We then find ourselves react-
ing in apparently irrational ways, much to the amazement of
those around us. If the raw nerve is touched we suddenly erupt.
Most people who erupt hate themselves for it afterwards or just
feel silly. Losing control is unpleasant and can be frightening.
The occasional outburst may be a healthy way of letting off
steam, but if it becomes a routine event we, or someone else in
the family, will want change.

DIY EXERCISE: LOCATING AND TREATING THE RAW NERVE

Is there anything that sets *you* off? Often we are unaware of what makes us have outbursts. Identifying specific triggers helps us avoid exploding suddenly. We can then begin to think constructively about change.

• What does a family member have to say or do for you to 'see red'?
• Recall a recent outburst and remember what you said and did. How did this affect those around you?
• Think about why they were affected in this way?

**What you can do**
• Predict the next time you are likely to explode.
• Think about what you can do to avoid exploding:
  – make light of it
  – distract yourself with some other activity
  – avoid the situation altogether.
• Now discuss this openly with your family/partner.
• Ask the person not to set you off.
• Practise restraint.

**Silent eruptions**

How people erupt varies a great deal. There are those who get red in the face, become very angry, shout and scream, let off steam, and then cool down. Others look visibly tense and then burst into tears. And there are those whose skin 'erupts' – often in quite dramatic ways. Red marks on the neck, itching and blotches on other parts of the body and certain skin conditions are visible signs of a raw nerve being touched. Keeping feelings in can be very disabling. Chronic depression or a persistent psychosomatic symptom is the price many people pay for not 'letting it out'.

Frequently we fear that if we start to unburden ourselves we won't be able to stop, as the distress is so overwhelming. People say: 'If I talk about this I will get so upset . . . I won't be able to control myself' or 'Once I start talking about it I won't be able to stop crying'. Clearly, if someone is terrified of voicing important feelings, then caution is necessary. If the person has been sitting on an emotional time bomb for years then the 'explosion' has to be controlled. This may require a 'bomb disposal expert' (possibly from outside the family), perhaps a really good friend or therapist with whom the person has a close, trusting relationship.

Talking to someone one trusts makes it possible to voice fragile feelings without being terrified that the other person is going to be overwhelmed or bored. Many people are unable to trust anybody with their distress because they fear being rejected, badly thought of, ridiculed or gossiped about. Moreover, some people worry that they might lose their friends if they flood them with all their worries. This is why they may seek out therapists whom they pay to listen to their distress.

Simply having someone there to listen to what nobody else wants to listen to can provide some relief. But, apart from this, therapy or counselling can help people look at familiar situations in a new light. Most therapists are unlikely to give straightforward advice. Instead they will help their clients to look at their own predicament from different perspectives. This can lead to the clients seeing new ways of tackling their problems and testing these out, first in the safety of the consulting room, and later with family and friends.

## ARGUMENTS

### How arguments start
It is possible to argue about literally anything and everything, including whether a particular discussion is in fact an argument or not:

> A: *'Stop arguing.'*
> B: *'I am not arguing, I am making a point?'*
> A: *'Oh nonsense, you* are *arguing. You always argue!'*
> B: *'Why is it so impossible to have a proper discussion with you?'*
> A: *'See what I mean!'*

Some arguments are one-off events; others are repetitive and highly predictable. Many arguments are about apparently petty things; few are about really deep issues. In most families there are certain situations when it seems almost impossible *not* to argue: for instance, when deciding on a family outing or talking about money. These and other arguments are routine events in every family.

How do arguments start? Most of us have plenty of experience of being in the midst of a family row. We tend to believe that someone else started it all. But of course that is exactly what the other person thinks. One of the oldest arguments of all is about who started the argument in the first place:

> A: *'You provoked me.'*
> B: *'I didn't say a word.'*
> A: *'It's the way you look at me.'*
> B: *'What are you talking about?*
>    *You are provoking me now...'*

Often it is impossible to determine who started the argument, but we all know how many of them begin:

> *'You never listen to me!'*
> *'Why do you always pick on me?'*
> *'You never believe what I say.'*
> *'You are always so untidy.'*

The words 'always' or 'never' almost inevitably provoke a heated response. When this is followed by 'Yes I do' or 'No you don't', such an exchange is guaranteed to go on for quite a while. Walking out on the argument means missing out on 'having the last word'. Almost everyone wants to have the last word, as each person believes that they are more right than the other. Of course, one can always choose not to reply to another person's last word, but that seems like backing down.

**Physical arguments**
The more one person says one thing, the more the other says the opposite. An argument, however petty its cause, can easily

escalate, with each party becoming more entrenched in his or her position. Such arguments frequently end not just in screaming matches but in violence.

One strategy many people employ is to fall silent during an argument or to act deaf, or both. Not being heard or not being replied to sometimes stops an argument, but it is just as likely to enrage the other person and can lead to a physical confrontation. Thankfully most people are able to anticipate this and storm out. When a person storms out during an argument he or she may see this as the only way of avoiding hitting out or being hit – or both.

When words no longer work, people may resort to fists to evoke a response. There are families where the arguments

---

### DIY EXERCISE: SLOW-MOTION REPLAY

When we watch a video we may wish to study how a particular scene evolved. To do this, we wind the tape back and watch the same scene a few times, possibly in slow motion.

- Similarly it is possible to replay, in one's mind, an imaginary video of a violent argument. To do this, start the 'film' with the last scene, when things came to a head.
- Try to identify what happened immediately before that. Go back, step by step, and write down the whole sequence – back to front.
- Now find a point in the sequence when you could have taken evasive action and think about the effect this might have had on the other person.
  Evasive action might consist of:
  – changing one's tone of voice
  – backing off or backing down
  – becoming playful and defusing the situation by distracting the other person
  – leaving the room or house altogether.
- The next time you find yourself in one of these routine arguments that habitually result in violence, try and follow your findings and stop the sequence in time.

---

routinely lead to physical confrontations. Essentially this is because people are no longer able to listen to one another. 'She drove me to it . . . she wouldn't listen' is the lame excuse given by the wifebeater, as if her alleged behaviour could for a moment excuse his violent action.

What can people do to avoid physical arguments? Both parties will be only too aware of the sequence of events that usually precedes violence. By the time someone says 'If you don't stop I'm going to hit you' it is often already too late. Spotting danger signals in good time is very important to protect oneself and others. This may sometimes involve extreme measures, such as calling the police or leaving the house.

Unfortunately police frequently do not intervene in what they tend to label 'domestic disputes' – even if these are highly explosive. However in recent years several police forces have set up domestic violence units which can give advice and practical help on how to keep safe and how to use the law to protect oneself. Sadly, lawyers often recommend that their clients should not leave the family home as this might threaten their rights to reside there in the long term. Whilst this advice may at times be legally correct, from a physical safety and emotional welfare point of view it is often very risky.

### Stopping arguments

We have already seen how difficult it can be to stop routine arguments. In a full-blown argument, any attempt to be rational is usually too late. Saying 'Oh dear, we're behaving just like children . . . Can't *you* see that?' is unlikely to halt an argument. Similarly, it is useless to pretend to give in or play the martyr. Theatrical declamations, such as 'It's all my fault', are more likely to refuel a dying conflict.

The only thing which might work is a climbdown which involves a genuine recognition of one's fallibility or wrongness, but this needs a lot of practice. Moreover, honesty and humility are not always rewarded, particularly if your opponent, after your admission, gives you the final stab: 'It's no good apologizing . . . You have done this for years and I cannot see that you will ever change . . .'

The temptation to respond in kind is almost irresistible, but even if you bite your tongue and reply 'I want to change' you could well elicit the implacable response 'But you won't'.

At this point your resolve may snap and the argument could flare up again: 'Yes I will' – 'No you won't' . . .

In short, it is extremely difficult to stop arguments because they so often follow a set pattern and reflect the two parties' fixed views of each other.

### Why some families 'need' arguments

Most families sometimes 'need' to have arguments in order to air problems, clarify relationships or even provide proof of love and concern. It is only when arguments happen routinely that one begins to question whether they are really needed. Some families are addicted to arguments. For them, regular arguing gives a sense of purpose to their lives. But most routine arguing is a way of drawing attention to some 'unfinished business' and it often takes place at family reunions.

> *Take the Brown family and their annual Christmas family get-together. The three grown-up 'children' and their respective families spend every Christmas with their ageing parents. It is usually only a few minutes before the first family row starts. The siblings fight with one another, as they always used to. Their parents tell them that it seems as if time has not moved on, but this has little effect. Old feuds resurface and although everyone secretly vows not to have a repeat performance next time round, things are no different the following year.*
>
> *Such rows paradoxically prove the strength of family ties and serve to reassure everybody, painful though it may be, that deep down nothing has really changed. At the same time everyone dreads the next Christmas and hopes to get rid of this 'unfinished business' once and for all.*

Most people would be reluctant to admit that violence and physical arguments were at the centre of their family life. Yet this is not at all uncommon. How can any family possibly 'need' to relate in this way? It may seem paradoxical, but physical confrontation is often the only way a person can feel loved.

---

DIY EXERCISE: 4 MINUTES EACH

---

To stop arguments or prevent them from escalating, something entirely different needs to happen – something so 'out of character' that it cannot be mistaken for more of the same. A good technique to try is '4 minutes each' (or 3 or 5 minutes – or any other time limit).

- During a time of calm each person agrees that, as an experiment over the course of a week, the next time there is a conflict one or both will say the magic words '4 minutes each'.
- This will be a cue for one person to say all he or she wants to say in 4 minutes flat and for the other to listen and not say a word.
- After 4 minutes it's the other person's turn.
- After that each person has 'the right to reply' – 4 minutes each.
- After that 4 minutes of silence have to be kept by both parties. No 'last words' are allowed.
- The ritual lasts exactly 20 minutes and should be timed rigorously. In the unlikely event that one of the parties runs out of ammunition, he or she should still be allocated the full time.
- Following this ritual, both parties should encourage one another to behave as spontaneously as possible – including reverting to their old-style of argument if they must.

*Mary, in her thirties, had a succession of violent partners, each of whom physically abused her. All her friends despaired about her apparent addiction to men who beat her up. When talking about it she would relate it back to her childhood when she felt she was only shown love when she had done something wrong. First she would be physically punished by her parents. Later they would feel remorseful about having hurt her. Then they would hug her, comforting her and telling her how much they really loved her. Mary 'learned' that something bad had to happen before she was entitled to love.*

*In her relationships with men she experienced something quite similar and she particularly enjoyed 'making up' after arguments or fights. Like many people, Mary had unfortunately grown up only experiencing closeness through an exchange of violence and the remorse felt afterwards. For her, physical confrontation had become a prerequisite for love.*

To break this cycle and to come to the realization that violence does not equal love can often seem an impossibly hard task. At times family therapy may be helpful in enabling such people to practise being in close physical contact with their child or partner when he or she is 'good'. This could happen whilst engaged in pleasurable activities, such as games, where positive exchanges can be encouraged.

Most children become excellent 'co-therapists', as they prefer to have a good rather than a bad time with their parents. On the whole they will tend to 'reward' their parents for being nice to them. This does not happen overnight, as children also like

testing their parents and parents may then give up all too easily. Once some more lasting changes have been made between a parent and child, the parents will start connecting with their own feelings of disappointment about how they were treated as children and realize that past disappointment can get in the way of having a good time with one's own children in the present.

## MALIGNANT ALLIANCES

So far we have considered how arguments can start and stop and what role they can play in family life. Now it's time to look a little more closely at some of their main causes.

It is only natural for anyone involved in an argument to look for an ally. Temporary alliances between different family members are a natural part of family life. A sister may at one time support her brother's wish to stay over with his best friend. At another time she may gang up with her mother against the lazy men (father and brother) who never do any housework. The parents in turn may back each other when it comes to laying down the law against smoking, but not on other issues. Such shifting alliances are signs of a healthy, flexible family.

However when two people join forces permanently against a third, we talk about a malignant alliance. Such alliances can cause a lot of trouble in the family, if two of its members constantly support one another and leave the third feeling isolated and beleaguered. Some other family members may then be tempted to join the other side, in an attempt to redress the balance and restabilize the family. This is how feuds are born.

People's initial motives for forming 'two-against-one' alliances are not always bad. A son may want to give support to his depressed and neglected mother; a mother may wish to protect her daughter against her excessively strict father. In the short term there may be comfort and safety in numbers, but there are dangers in permanently aligning with one person. These are particularly obvious when it comes to forming a strong alliance with a child; when the ally is not present, the child has to face his or her opponent alone. Without support the child is also that much more vulnerable because he or she has not developed ways of coping alone.

## Alliances between young and old

Although fewer families nowadays live with, or close to, grandparents, many alliances still involve them. In such alliances the children may be manoeuvred effectively against another member of the family. For instance, a grandmother may spoil her grandchild to demonstrate to her daughter what an inadequate mother she is. When the mother accuses Granny of stirring things up, the grandchild rushes to Nan's defence. This infuriates the mother further and she punishes them both by stopping the grandchild from seeing his or her grandmother.

In some alliances children literally start to behave like a ventriloquist's dummy and chillingly impersonate their 'master's voice'. Children rarely choose to take on such roles but are often manoeuvred into them. Such scenarios point to deep-seated problems, with the child often behaving in bizarre ways.

*Johnny, ten years of age, always sided with his father against his mother. Mrs Green had got used to this and felt sorry for him because she thought he was getting caught up in their marital problems. But when her son started talking to her in his father's tone of voice, with similar pauses and accompanied by identical gestures, she became alarmed.*

*Johnny did this particularly when his father was away on business trips and he would call her then by her first name, just the way her husband did. Mrs Green felt that Johnny's father was present even when he was absent and that he had instructed their son to be his deputy. Johnny dutifully reported back to his father on his return, usually in a grave voice, describing his mother's conduct in detail and consulting his 'notes'.*

Malignant alliances are not always 'two-against-one'. They can also be 'one-between-two'. In this case one person, often a child, gets caught between warring factions.

DIY EXERCISE: SPOTTING AND STOPPING
MALIGNANT ALLIANCES

You may be part of an alliance or you may see an alliance between others. If you feel that this is the case, it's worth attempting to confirm your feelings.

**Spotting malignant alliances**
• Identify possible alliance(s) in your family – possibly with the help of the relationship map (see page 15).
• Now look for some of the following signs:
  – secretive behaviour: excluding people, whispering, stopping a conversation as soon as a third person enters the room
  – ventriloquist's dummy: a child imitating an adult's voice or behaviour, always backing one parent's position
  – indirect communication: enlisting the support of a third party, e.g. 'Ask A, he'll tell you that he agrees with me'
  – a family member behaving unnaturally or in a constrained way with a specific third person
  – a family member who avoids being alone with you.

**Stopping malignant alliances**
• If you are part of a malignant alliance:
  – list the negative effects the alliance has and on whom
  – consider what would happen if the alliance was weakened in some way
  – tell the other party that from now on there are no more secrets
  – do not pass on messages for others or explain their positions
  – deal with people face to face: do not tell anyone to pass messages on for you
  – set an example: be open about your views and discuss them freely with everybody
  – do not engage in secretive behaviour, however tempting it may be.

John:  'You were there, Bob, so you know what happened . . . Who started the argument . . . It was Mary, wasn't it?'

Mary:  'Oh come on, Bob has eyes and ears . . . he knows how you wind me up . . . Isn't that right, Bob?'

John:  'You're trying to influence Bob again. He has a mind of his own . . . haven't you, Bob? You know that Mary started it!'

Mary:  'Here we go again . . . It's you who tries to brainwash him . . . Let's hear from Bob what he thinks.'

Referees are meant to be neutral, but this is difficult at the best of times and impossible when one is related to both factions. If Bob, referee in the making, does not overtly back John, he will be accused of backing Mary. And the same charge will be levelled by the other party. He is in a 'no win' position. Whatever he does, he gets it in the neck. He is torn between two warring factions or 'triangulated'. And being part of a triangle is a rotten predicament.

Bob could refuse to get drawn into their argument. He could simply say 'It's between the two of you, leave me out of it' and walk out. But some Bobs – and many Bills, Christines and Peters – cannot walk out because they happen to be the children of these two adults and therefore dependent on them. And even if Bob were an adult he might be afraid that, if he left, John and Mary would have a physical fight.

Some people spend their lives as referees, without ever being allowed to blow the whistle. Sadly, children often get caught in the crossfire. They become 'stand-ins': if you cannot get through to your wife directly why not use your son as a weapon? In this way the child becomes a buffer in the parental relationship.

## SCAPEGOATING

Anyone familiar with the game of snooker will know that, in order to pocket a ball, you need to cue another one. In some families it is amazingly easy for one person to cue another one and set a whole earthquake in motion. We have all come across the little boy who winds up his older sister when nobody else is in the room. She eventually lashes out at him, precisely at the point when their mother opens the door – with predictable results. With luck, next time round the mother will open the door sooner and then the little brother will get the blame.

Getting blamed occasionally is very different from being fixed in the role of family scapegoat. Most families do not require scapegoats because they acknowledge that everyone can get things wrong from time to time. Thus there is no need for just one person to be blamed for virtually everything that goes wrong. In the old days a 'scape-goat' was sacrificed to God to atone for the sins of a group. Nowadays this happens more subtly . . .

## Why some families 'need' scapegoats

It is only human for people to view themselves, from time to time, as the victims of an awful husband, nagging wife, or a family vendetta. When things go badly in a relationship or family it is easier if one person takes the blame. Sometimes that person may be outside the immediate family and everyone bands together to fight the common enemy.

The enemy could be a doctor who is blamed for the failed treatment of a depressed family member, with the implication that he may even have caused the illness. It could be a school which is held responsible for having 'taught' a child how to swear. Or it could be a grandparent who is seen as having caused everyone's misery.

Whoever the external enemy, the net effect is that the family sticks together, raising the question of what would happen if the enemy outside was removed . . . When that happens someone has to take the blame for what has gone wrong and it is usually the most vulnerable person in the family who gets stuck with this unrewarding role.

Scapegoats come in many different shapes. One extreme is 'the villain of the piece'. He (it is usually a man) has seemingly unrivalled power to unite a whole family against him, thereby indirectly preserving or promoting family togetherness. Another extreme is 'the madman' who, incidentally, is marginally more likely to be a woman than a man. In this scenario everyone is eager to point out that 'She cannot help it, it's not her fault . . . She is just mad . . . you know' (with meaningful glances exchanged, usually behind the person's back). People have a tendency to feel sorry for the mad one. Mad or bad – both types improve cohesion amongst the rest of the family. The family scapegoat can also serve to deflect pressure from another person who is in trouble.

> *David, aged twelve, lived with his sister, mother and grandmother. Men had never been very popular in this family and tended to get thrown out soon after they had fathered a child. They were seen as aggressive and unreliable. Not surprisingly, David soon acquired these 'male characteristics' in the eyes of his immediate family. His school had quite a different view and his reports regularly emphasized how gentle and trustworthy he was.*
>
> *This was in marked contrast to his sister Jenny's performance at school: she tended to get involved in fights and had few friends. When the school contacted their mother about Jenny's behaviour, David got the blame. Mother claimed that David had set a bad example and taught his sister how to fight. She concluded that he was just like his father and that women and girls generally had no wish to be aggressive. None of David's actions or words could persuade her otherwise. Eventually the self-fulfilling prophecy came true, and he started behaving more and more disruptively in the home.*

In some families it is virtually impossible to escape from the role of scapegoat. For the scapegoat to ask 'Why do you always blame *me* for everything that goes wrong?' is a waste of time. The rest of the family joins forces, citing numerous examples of typically mad or bad behaviour – leaving out the many other occasions that do not prove the point. Being wrongly accused eventually leads the scapegoat to commit precisely those 'crimes' he has been blamed for. 'I'm taking the blame so I might as well do it . . .' he thinks, thereby proving the rest of the family 'right'. No amount of proving one's worth is sufficient since the rest of the family will always be watching and waiting for the next slip-up.

Other family members project their own shortcomings or

unpleasant thoughts on to scapegoats. What they do not like about themselves gets located in someone else who can then be attacked. They then feel better.

If a family needs a scapegoat for its survival then it will look for a new one if the old one leaves. There are families who live in an ongoing relay race. Unable to live without a 'baddie', the scapegoat baton is passed from person to person.

---

DIY EXERCISE: AVOIDING THE SCAPEGOAT'S ROLE

Is someone being scapegoated in your family? Consider the following points:
- Is there someone in your family who gets blamed more often than others?
- Why is that and how did he/she get into that position?
- List what he/she does to stay in that role.
- What do other family members do to maintain the person in that role?
- Try to remember whether there was ever a time when someone else was a scapegoat.
- Consider what would be better/worse in your family if there was no scapegoat.

**What you can do:**
- Consider carrying out an experiment for one week.
- Decide that for this week you will not blame the scapegoat.
- Whenever something goes wrong, blame yourself – or if that gets too much – blame someone else, but not the scapegoat.
- Carefully monitor everybody's reactions.
- Enlist at least one other person's help for this project.
- Discuss your findings at the end of the week.
- Repeat the experiment again – if you really want to break the pattern.

---

*The Smith family had seven children. They seemed to be no trouble when young, but each appeared to become a problem to their parents on reaching adolescence. The oldest was blamed for*

*the bad behaviour of the younger ones and charged with 'setting
a bad example'. When he left home at sixteen it was his sister's
turn to be accused of teaching her younger brothers and sisters
how to misbehave. No sooner had she left home than the next
oldest was charged with disrupting family life. The parents
remained united and felt blameless, whilst the next child
prepared to take the baton.*

Such relay races are not consciously planned; they seem to
happen automatically. Sometimes leaving home seems the
only solution. Scapegoats cannot usually take on the whole
family single-handed; they may need assistance from another
family member. Scapegoats need allies – someone to join them
openly in their struggle against collective injustice. That person is often outside the immediate family. They could be a
family friend, a teacher or a therapist – someone who validates
the scapegoat's own perception of himself or herself and therefore becomes a trusted ally.

**The family fool**
A milder form of the scapegoat, located somewhere between
the extremes of 'mad' and 'bad', is the family fool. Fools need
not be foolish. (Many of Shakespeare's fools were wiser than
his heroes and heroines.) In some families any tension immediately gets dispersed by Mr Fool-in-Residence making silly
gestures or ridiculous remarks. However, although often initially appreciated, such behaviour is eventually condemned.
'You never take anyone seriously,' other family members may
say, or 'it is impossible to have a proper discussion with you.'

Is it worth acting the fool? At times it is extremely handy to
have someone who is able to distract the family from more
serious matters. As a solution to an immediate problem this
can be a very good way of coping. However, if the fool still
behaves foolishly when the crisis is over, this initial solution can
become a problem in its own right.

*Uncle John had always been regarded as eccentric by the rest of
his large family. Much liked, he was also the object of
considerable ridicule. He wore funny clothes, spoke with a most*

*peculiar accent and often gesticulated in a fairly absurd way.*
*However everyone agreed that he was a very kind man.*
*Unattached, he seemed to live nowhere and everywhere.*

*He had a knack of turning up whenever any of his brother's*
*and sister's families were in trouble. First he cheered them up.*
*But then he started annoying the older generation who blamed*
*him for setting a bad example to their children. The children*
*would then defend him, forming alliances which annoyed their*
*parents even more. Uncle John would eventually be asked to*
*leave but forgiven, as 'He is a bit of a fool'. The family then felt*
*intact, for a while, until the next time round.*

The risk in acting the fool for too long is that the act turns into
a permanent way of behaving. But behind the clown's mask
there is often a very sad face; trapped in his role, acting the fool
is the only way he knows of relating to the family.

It is important to release the family fool from his or her
unrewarding role. Family and friends can train themselves to
develop selective hearing: to listen more to the serious communications rather than just the jokes. It may be unwise to give up
laughing altogether, however, as it can deprive the fool of his
familiar role and make him redouble his efforts. Paying more
attention to the less funny side of his or her personality gives
the message that one is genuinely interested in the person
behind the jolly mask. Then again, if the family needs a fool,
perhaps to distract from some serious issues, one needs to be
on the look-out for someone else slipping into this role . . .

## LOVING PEOPLE TO DEATH

Families which contain a scapegoat can appear terribly cruel to
outsiders. By contrast, very caring families seem sheer paradise. Yet to be caring is one thing; to be overbearing is another.
When overprotectiveness becomes an entrenched behaviour
pattern, people can feel suffocated.

*Stephanie went on hunger strike when she was fifteen. Her*
*parents had been very proud of what a close family they were.*

*Up to then Stephanie had been able to tell her parents everything and her mother often boasted that she knew her daughter inside out. In fact, she believed she knew exactly what Stephanie was feeling and thinking.*

*Stephanie did not appear to object to Mother's constant mind-reading and learned not to complete her sentences, as 'Mum knows anyway'. She never raised any objections to her mother and father reading her private diary and then discussing it at dinner with the rest of the family. Her father would confirm that 'We have no secrets in this family'. As they were such a 'close' family, it was not possible for Stephanie to challenge this total lack of privacy directly. Instead she started sealing her lips, talking less and less and eventually refusing to eat. This seemed a way of establishing an identity of her own and proving her independence.*

*Faced with their daughter's dramatic deterioration, the parents sought help. Their GP sent them to a child psychiatrist who saw the whole family. Here Stephanie finally started talking about how difficult she found it to think of anything as being her own, be it her room, her ambitions, her thoughts – even her body. She felt she had to go on a hunger strike to protest. She could see no other way of making a clear statement, one that would not be modified by her parents.*

*Her parents were shocked: what had happened to their nice little girl? Stephanie felt both guilty and angry. She had never spoken to her parents like this before. When her mother said that surely Stephanie did not mean what she said, she exploded: 'You twist everything I say . . . I am me . . . let me be me . . .'. This was the beginning of a long struggle back towards health, a struggle that was painful not only for Stephanie but also for her parents who gradually had to learn to accept that their daughter was a person in her own right, with her own mouth and her own mind.*

Such self-starvation is an example of how too much love can sometimes kill. Ironically, living with an anorexic often leads families to redouble their efforts to get through to their child, forcing her to eat. The ensuing battle can provide an important opportunity to establish boundaries as the young person fights back against parental intrusiveness. It is a positive sign for her (or occasionally him) to say 'no', though hopefully the battle can gradually be shifted on to less dangerous ground – for instance fighting for a lock on the bedroom door.

Without boundaries people live in each other's pockets and find it difficult to see themselves as independent individuals. Their development is slowed down. This type of over-closeness is known as 'enmeshment'. So-called enmeshed families are sometimes the envy of families who are falling apart – where there is little contact between the various family members. However, many children from enmeshed families envy their peers who live in these more 'disengaged' families. It seems that the grass is always greener on the other side . . .

Few families show all the characteristics of pure enmeshment – most present a mixture of features, some of which suggest

---

DIY EXERCISE:  USEFUL BOUNDARIES IN THE HOME

Feeling trapped in the family hinders personal growth. Here are a few tips on how to free ourselves by creating boundaries in the home:
- Respect each other's privacy (don't listen to other people's telephone calls, don't read other people's post or diaries).
- Refrain from mind-reading.
- Try not to finish other people's sentences.
- Assume that people have their own brains and voices. Encourage them to use these.
- Encourage constructive dissent inside the family.
- Practise saying 'That's *my* business' or 'That's got nothing to do with you'. Say it when it's appropriate.
- Consider putting locks on the bathroom and toilet doors – as a symbolic act. They need never be used if you do not wish to use them.
- Avoid caring for family members as if they were your 'patients'.

closeness and others considerable distance. Family maps (see Chapter 1) reveal such differences. Everyone seems to need space – at least some of the time. Yet there are those who find it very difficult to ask for such breathing space. They allow themselves to feel guilty about being unable to meet the endless demands of their relatives. In extreme cases guilt can effectively stop a person from ever daring to absent himself or herself from the bosom, or prison, of the family.

A common scenario is the 'dutiful daughter' who has the life-time job of looking after her parents or other needy members of the family. Somewhat paradoxically, her brothers may encourage their sister to have a life of her own whilst at the same time putting her under subtle pressure to keep an eye on the parents. This faces the dutiful daughter with a dilemma: if she pursues her own life she risks being thought selfish. If she remains the dutiful daughter she may be sacrificing her own happiness and find herself feeling lost and lonely when the parents die. Clearly it is important for all the siblings to get together and have an open discussion about this problem. This is common sense, but surprisingly rare. Apart from the dutiful daughter, the current arrangement may suit everyone else – so why discuss it?!

## PUTTING PEOPLE DOWN

Most people have plenty of experience both of being put down and of putting others down. When this behaviour becomes entrenched, it can be very destructive. The motivation for putting others down is obvious: one-upmanship. If A is down, then B is, relatively speaking, one-up. One-upmanship is not a purely male pursuit, though it is certainly more common amongst the allegedly stronger sex.

Strange though it may seem, whilst the majority of people appear to prefer the one-up position, there are also those who see the advantages of being one-down. In fact being one-down can often give you more power than being one-up. Learned helplessness, for instance, is a very effective way of getting others to do things for you.

'I don't know how to change a light bulb' is the appeal of a damsel in distress to a knight in shining armour, who may boast, with disarming pride, that 'I don't know how to cook.' Relationships based on such convenient, mutual arrangements are in line with commonly held ideas about male and female roles. Supposing she did a course on light-bulb-changing and became very good at it, where would this leave our knight? He would no longer have a role in her life and might even lose his rights to her cooking!

On a more serious note, down-putting if performed routinely, amounts to no less than emotional abuse.

> Father: *'You are so thick . . . Look at your sister, she is so much cleverer.'*
> Mother: *'You are so clumsy . . . You'll never be good with your hands.'*

Such comments, if made over and over again, leave anybody's self esteem dented. Some people, for one reason or another, get addicted to being disqualified in this way. The advantages are obvious: if you put yourself down first, you beat others to it. *You* say it before *they* can. Even more strikingly, if you put yourself down subtly, other people will have to rush to your defence and try to build up your confidence.

Consider this common, seemingly endless, dialogue:

> A: *'I'm hopeless at . . .'*
> B: *'No, you're not.'*
> A: *'But I cannot do . . .'*
> B: *'I think you've forgotten what you did so well the other day . . .'*
> A: *'Thanks for reminding me . . . You are so good to me . . . I don't deserve this.'*
> B: *'Of course you do. You are a very nice and competent person.'*
> A: *(sighing) 'I wish that was true.'*
> B: *'It is.'*

In such see-saw relationships one person is down when the other tends to be up. If *she* is optimistic, *he* tends to be more cautious. If *she* is depressed, *he* tries to cheer her up. If he gets drunk, she may want to stay sober. But tomorrow it may be the other way round ... Complementing each other's needs is important, as long as people don't get stuck in extreme positions for ever.

## DRIVING PEOPLE MAD

There are almost too many theories to explain why people go crazy. Some hold specific genes or chromosomes responsible. Others blame viruses, the seasons, chemicals or hormones. Here we shall examine the 'family factor' which can contribute to someone losing his or her grip on reality. There is little doubt that people have the ability to drive each other totally crazy – usually without wishing to do so.

### Relationship traps: the double bind

Some families lay relationship traps without realizing it. Once caught, the victim finds it very difficult to escape. The 'double bind' is one such trap and it takes four ingredients for a person to get entangled in it:

– one message at a verbal level ('don't do that')
– another message at a tonal or body language level, contradicting the first ('don't listen to anything I say')
– a rule against commenting on the contradiction: anyone pointing out that there is a double message will have their sanity or powers of perception called into question ('I don't know what you're talking about')
– a 'captive audience' who cannot get away from the family: for instance a child or seriously ill adult.

Here's an example of a double bind in practice.
*A father feels exhausted by looking after his child. Instead of saying 'go away, leave me in peace, I am sick and tired of you', he tells his daughter: 'I want you to do something nice. Go and see your friend. You are very bored here alone with me. I want you to go and play with your friend.'*
*If the child is pleased about what she takes to be her father's show*

*51*

*of parental concern, she may want to give him a hug to say*
*'Thanks'. Father, as he is already sick and tired of his daughter,*
*will very likely pull back from her embrace.*
*She will pick up on this and ask*
*'Why do you move away? Don't you love me?' and get upset.*
*This in turn will make him angry: 'Can't you leave me in peace,*
*for once!'*
*But if she then questions his anger: 'Why are you angry now?*
*What have I done?', he will get even angrier with her: 'I'm not*
*angry!!!'*
*In this way she will get punished for trying to untangle the*
*contradictory messages.*

Such messages can come from one person or, characteristically, from two, where following the instructions of one parent means not obeying the commands of the other. As a dependent child or young person usually cannot afford to fall out with either parent, the only remaining option may seem to be to act strange or even 'mad'. This means the child is no longer taken seriously and is therefore freed from having to come down on one side or the other.

Many interactions between parent(s) and children have some ingredients of the double bind. So why aren't we all mad? What appears to make a difference is the frequency and consistency with which all this happens. The more often parents distort their real feelings in the ways described, the more confused the child will become. If this goes on over years then the young person no longer knows what is true and what is not. In order to learn to trust it is vitally important for children – and adults – to be able to identify the correct message.

What can the 'victim' do? One possibility is to leave home, cutting off all channels of communication. Many young people who suddenly disappear, often without saying goodbye, see this as their only chance to get out of the family web. Not surprisingly, such dramatic escapes often fail, as the young person – confused by years of double messages – feels that he or she cannot cope on their own. The young person returns home doubly defeated and with even less hope of ever getting away.

Another possibility is to develop selective deafness – learning to switch off whenever double messages are received. However, such selective deafness carries the risk of ignoring other communication as well and can lead to young people locking themselves in their rooms for weeks or months.

A common way of surviving relationship traps is for the 'victim' to find a trustworthy attachment figure. This can be a grandparent, an aunt or uncle, or a family friend. Such at attachment helps to prove that there are people who say what they mean and that it is possible to talk straight. This places pathological family communications in context, as only one of a number of ways of conducting relationships.

**Getting confused**
Everyone gets confused from time to time. We think we remember something happening but someone else who was present totally denies that it ever took place. We are perplexed: how is this possible?

> He: *'I never said that.'*
> She: *'Yes, of course you did.'*
> He: *'You're imagining things, dear.'*

*She: 'No, I'm not.'*
*He: 'I think you're hearing things I would never dream of saying.'*
*She: 'Are you telling me that I am mad?'*

This is a familiar argument – we frequently blame our poor or selective memories for many of our misunderstandings. Two people's recollection of the same event can be so different that a third person listening finds it impossible to connect them. But all this seems fairly normal. It is somewhat less normal to set out deliberately to drive someone else mad – either to assert one's control over that person or to get rid of them altogether. Hitchcock gave us a memorable film portrayal of a murderous husband confusing his unsuspecting wife by making certain items appear and disappear again.

*'Have you seen my gaslighter?' she asks, minutes after she put it down on the table. 'Haven't seen it for months, dear' is his reply, having just removed and pocketed it. A few minutes later he secretly places it back on the table. 'Ah, there it is. . .' she sighs, whereupon, in an unseen moment, he removes it again. 'Where is it?' she asks, sounding alarmed. 'Where is what, dear?' he replies innocently. 'The gaslighter, it was here just a few minutes ago.' He can now use his punchline: 'Are you sure you're not seeing things, dear?'*

Whilst ordinary people are usually less calculating than Hitchcock's characters, many of us will from time to time resort to 'gaslighting' tactics, perhaps without even realizing it, and semi-deliberately misplace items or memories. The (often unconscious) reason for doing so is that one can feel and look comparatively sane in the presence of a 'mad' person. If such maddening medicine is prescribed regularly then it is only a matter of weeks before the 'patient' feels the effects.

Confusion can often be created by a tone of voice which contradicts the words used. The word 'dear' is a good example. Though apparently a term of affection, a bitter or sarcastic tone can endow it with all sorts of nuances, ranging from contempt to total hatred.

DIY EXERCISE: SAY WHAT YOU MEAN

When it comes to serious family business it is best to be straight – otherwise you risk not being taken seriously. Some people have become addicted to sarcasm and irony or are habitually very indirect. This is often related to how they have been brought up: they may come from families where it was unwise or dangerous to say what you meant. Useful though this may once have been, it almost inevitably becomes a handicap in later life.

If you want to change the pattern, practise the following – first by yourself and then with a person you trust. This could be a family member or perhaps, to be on the safe side, a very good friend.

- Think of an awkward subject you have difficulty in talking about directly (e.g. to do with interfering in-laws, your teenage children's sexual experimentation, or your partner's depression).
- Imagine that the person concerned is sitting in front of you.
- Think of what you would like to say if you were entirely truthful.
- Consider the different ways in which you could do this, and imagine the other person's responses.
- Now choose which would convey what you want to say in the most straightforward way.
- Consider the risks of doing so: what is the worst that could happen?
- Experiment and see whether your worst case scenario actually happens.

## THE DANGERS OF GIVING AND TAKING ADVICE

This chapter has described entrenched relationship patterns and ways of changing them. Whether people do indeed want to alter any of their daily routines depends entirely on whether *they* regard them as sufficiently annoying or destructive. We must avoid judging other people's relationships by our own standards or prescribing for others the medicine that works for us.

For instance, take the familiar question of whether two partners are better off together or apart. What advice can an outsider possibly give? Some partners often stay in what appear to be very morbid relationships, with both parties seemingly addicted to emotional pain. Others get married, intending to live happily ever after, and it comes as a shock when they separate a few weeks later. It seems impossible to give any advice on whether couples should stay together or not.

Moreover, a lot of advice has a counter-productive effect even though, or perhaps because, it is so often based on apparent common sense. People frequently seem to do precisely the opposite of what a well-meaning friend advises them. And, to complicate matters further, not giving any advice doesn't seem to help either. Encouraging others to find their own solutions by asking repetitive and non-committal 'What do *you* think?' type questions may work if you are a professional therapist, but not when you are a friend or family member.

Here are a few hints on handling this sort of situation:

- Be careful about giving others straight advice on whether or not they should stay in a relationship.
- Help them instead to weigh up the advantages and disadvantages of change.
- Raise questions which enable them to find their own solutions to personal dilemmas – rather than prescribing answers.
- If you want advice yourself then ask other people, but do not take their advice simply because they have given it.
- Weigh up the different options and take responsibility for the one you choose.

The same goes for this book. The advice you choose to follow will depend on your personal circumstances and willingness to change. The DIY exercises and survival techniques are there to help raise your awareness of common but often painful ways of relating. Experiment, but don't go overboard: challenging and abandoning long-established routines, however strange they may appear, can be upsetting to some family members. At times professional help may be necessary.

## Chapter 3

# Changing family scripts

IN THIS CHAPTER WE LOOK AT:

•

## POSITIVE AND NEGATIVE FEEDBACK IN RELATIONSHIPS

•

## CHANGING THE WAY WE SAY THINGS

•

## CHOOSING THE RIGHT TIME AND PLACE TO SAY THINGS

•

## CHANGING FAMILIAR SCRIPTS

•

## FORECASTING AND PREPARING FOR FAMILY CRISES

A: *'It's always me who has to do the washing up.'*
B: *'You never let me do it in my own time.'*
A: *'You just leave it . . . I might as well do it myself.'*
B: *'But how can I ever do it if you do it before I have a chance?'*
A: *'You've had plenty of chances over the last fifteen years.'*
B: *'You just don't let me do the washing up because you like to complain.'*
A: *'Go on, do it then. Now.'*
B: *'You're so bossy. Can't you see that?'*
A: *'It's you who puts me in that position.'*

Families perfect scripts, usually over generations. They hand on to children their half-baked 'recipes' for everything from child-rearing practices to the making and breaking of relationships. Each successive generation tries to adopt a similar approach to life, thereby repeating the family script. Alternatively, in order to avoid their parents' mistakes, the next generation tries to correct a script handed to them and does quite the opposite. For example, if one felt smothered as a child one might try to give one's own offspring more independence.

Most people are not really aware that many of their actions are guided by a predictable script. Some family scripts, like certain theatre plays, are so successful that they seem to be performed for ever. *The Mousetrap* has now been running for more than forty years in London's West End. It is a classic murder mystery and the lines have always remained the same, though countless actors have died, divorced or given birth since it first started. Compared with real-life dramas, however, *The Mousetrap* is a one-day wonder. *The Marriage Trap*, for instance, is surely one of the longest-running shows on earth – with no single villain and no simple whodunnit solution. Many of us become stuck in our own plays and long to change the script. This chapter describes some ways of doing so.

## THE IMPORTANCE OF FEEDBACK

It is impossible not to respond to what other people say or do. Even if we decide to ignore what another person says, the decision not to respond is a response. Other people are in the same position – they respond to our responses to their responses and so on . . . we call this process 'feedback' and it is the engine that drives human communication.

For example, when Dad tells three-year-old Matthew that he has done well to put his toys away and Matthew does it again the next day he is responding positively to his dad's encouragement. Dad's subsequent smile feeds back to Matthew who now receives more positive feedback. At this point they are both involved in a positive loop. It's difficult to tell what comes first. Dad believes his praise has elicited more of Matthew's 'good' behaviour: when it spontaneously occurs, Dad reinforces it. Yet, it could be argued that Matthew has elicited Dad's positive comments by doing the 'right' thing.

Most of us thrive on what we call positive feedback – acknowledgement and praise for what we have done well. Consider this dialogue:

> *She: 'I love you.'*
> *He: 'I love you.'*
> *She: 'I have never loved anyone so much – ever.'*
> *He: 'I would never have imagined that I could love anyone so much.'*
> *She: 'Without your love I am nobody.'*
> *He: 'Without your love I am nothing.'*

Both partners give each other positive feedback and this is likely to make them both feel good. Positive remarks elicit positive responses and this is clearly a good thing. Is there ever a limit? Not until infatuation wears off.

For a third person listening to the couple's interchange, this mutual adoration may also have negative aspects: they become totally self-absorbed, forget the outside world, and may get quite inflated views of their own importance. Moreover, our observer might even get jealous as he listens to how much in

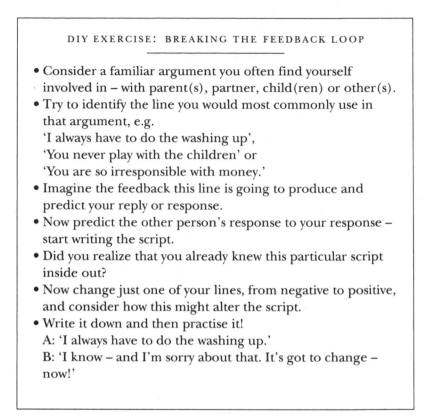

DIY EXERCISE: BREAKING THE FEEDBACK LOOP

- Consider a familiar argument you often find yourself involved in – with parent(s), partner, child(ren) or other(s).
- Try to identify the line you would most commonly use in that argument, e.g.
  'I always have to do the washing up',
  'You never play with the children' or
  'You are so irresponsible with money.'
- Imagine the feedback this line is going to produce and predict your reply or response.
- Now predict the other person's response to your response – start writing the script.
- Did you realize that you already knew this particular script inside out?
- Now change just one of your lines, from negative to positive, and consider how this might alter the script.
- Write it down and then practise it!
  A: 'I always have to do the washing up.'
  B: 'I know – and I'm sorry about that. It's got to change – now!'

love these two are, and this may well have a negative effect on him.

In short, it depends (as so often) on one's perspective: what is positive to some may be negative to others. For example, the young woman's mother may not like her daughter's boyfriend, and being aware of the extent of her infatuation with him may make her mother feel even more negative. When she tells her daughter about her mixed feelings the latter will probably see this as negative feedback – even though the mother believes that her response might be positive feedback for her daughter, in the long run. . . .

Negative feedback is very common: most arguments are based on it. Generally we hate negative feedback, although it can sometimes have a positive effect. When it bothers us too much we change our ways, if only so that we do not have to listen to any more of it. However the most common way of dealing with negative feedback is to respond in kind: if A criticizes B, then B criticizes A. One negative line elicits another, which triggers further verbal abuse, which results in more of the same.

Sometimes life seems to be made up of infinite negative feedback loops which all those involved would like to sever. But this is easier said than done. Addiction to the familiar is a common problem; the invisible record player needle gets stuck in the same groove.

Giving *unexpected* feedback makes it possible to break the pattern. If a person habitually says 'no' to everything, everyone will come to expect him to say 'no' all the time. Our lives are full of such familiar steps and turns worked out in advance in the endless dance of family warfare. Why do we go on and on, twisting and turning in familiar ways? Why not introduce the occasional new step or tune? Why not say 'yes' for a change?

## CHANGING THE WAY WE SAY OUR LINES

Adding a new line is only one way of breaking the feedback loop. We all know that it not only matters *what* people say, but also *how* they say it. We don't just listen to the verbal content. We also take in the tone, namely *how* the lines are delivered.

On the stage, at the opera or theatre, we become aware of a whole range of intonations and inflections, from *piano* to *fortissimo*, with pauses, or sarcastic or sad undertones, fast or slow deliveries. The tone crucially affects what is being said. The same words uttered very loudly can carry a totally different meaning from when they are whispered. Consider the following:

> *Dad (loud voice):* *'Jack, I cannot stand your mother.'*
> *Dad (whispers):* *'Jack, I cannot stand your mother.'*

The first communication is a direct message to Mother who is meant to hear it – Jack is simply being used to make the point. The second communication is secretive and sets up an alliance,

---

DIY EXERCISE: CHOOSING THE RIGHT TONE
---

- Decide what you want to say.
- Decide what sort of response you would like to get:
  – positive
  – negative
  – ambiguous.
- Select any tone from the list below:
  – calm
  – angry
  – sarcastic
  – injured
  – sad
  – happy.
- Which tone of voice is most likely to produce the response you want?
- So far you have conducted this experiment all by yourself, perhaps in front of a mirror, with nobody listening. Now you may want to pluck up courage and test it with a trusted friend.
- Be careful when you use the new tone(s) the first time within the family: you may get strong reactions . . .

---

making things potentially very awkward for Jack.

The tone in which a line is delivered can match its content – or not. A recently bereaved mother who tells her twenty-two-year-old son to 'Go out and enjoy yourself. Don't worry about me, I can look after myself' can speak with conviction and her son will believe her and go out and probably enjoy himself. But the same lines could be delivered by another mother, in a sad and reproachful voice, transmitting the underlying message that she would feel awful if he really were to leave her on her own. The effect on the son is fairly predictable: he will feel mixed up, resentful about staying at home and guilty about going out. As we have already seen, such double messages can eventually drive people mad.

## THE RIGHT TIME AND PLACE

It's not just what we say and how we say it that matters. Timing and context are also crucial.

**When to say it**

For example, do you wait until your partner has put his feet up before you tell him that you have made yet another dent in his precious car? Or do you tell him the bad news the moment he walks in from work? When is the best time to tell your wife that your mother has decided to come on holiday with you? Do you wait till the last minute?

People frequently choose the worst possible time to deliver important lines: 3 am, during the evening news, or whilst giving birth. As a result they either end up not being listened to or fuelling an already smouldering conflict. Such bad timing is rarely deliberate, although this charge is often levelled by the person on the receiving end: 'You are doing this on purpose, to wind me up. You always want to talk about important issues when I am watching the football.' But on the whole people aren't cool and calculating. They just want to be listened to.

So how can you get the timing right? Firstly, it is important to

---

### DIY EXERCISE: CHOOSING THE RIGHT TIME

- Decide what you want to say.
- Decide what kind of response you want.
- Choose the 'right' time:
  - when things are calm
  - when you are relaxed
  - when the other person can listen.
- Consider your delivery:
  - tone, speed, pauses, silences
  - leave space for the other person to reply.
- Choose a style of delivery to match the required response.
- Put it to the test with a fairly minor issue.
- Evaluate the result.

---

identify a time when your partner is not distracted, so that he or she can pay full attention. Secondly, people in a relaxed and receptive mood are more likely to listen. Thirdly, it is sometimes helpful to give some advance warning so that both partners can get in the right mood and prepare themselves for what is to come.

On occasions it may be important to set some regular time aside to discuss important matters. There are partners who are unlikely to listen to one another unless they book regular appointments. Bizarre though it may seem, this may even involve getting diaries or filofaxes out and finding a mutually convenient time. Booking regular times with one another is rarely a good long-term solution to relationship problems, but with couples who never have time for one another it may be a first step towards opening up the channels of communication.

**Where to say it**
*Where* you deliver your lines will also help to determine their impact. It is crucial to choose a good location and, to maximize the effect, make certain that all important members of the cast are present.

---

DIY EXERCISE: CHOOSING THE RIGHT PLACE

- Decide what you want to say.
- Decide what kind of response you want.
- Choose the 'right' place or situation:
  - just the two of you
  - with a third person present
  - in a public place
  - in the bathroom, bedroom or kitchen
  - outside, looking at a romantic sunset
  - inside, in the office.
- Choose a place to match the required response.
- Put it to the test and evaluate the result.

---

## WRITING NEW SCRIPTS

You now have the main tools for changing aspects of your family life – should you wish to do so. You have mapped your current family relationships, traced myths and secrets and

---

### DIY EXERCISE: CHANGING THE SCRIPT

Before changing scripts one needs to understand the problems that have created them.

**Understanding the script**
- Choose a familiar scenario, such as an argument or another relationship problem you want to change.
- Draw a relationship map (see page 13) and consider how it reflects the problem.
- Ask yourself what changes would need to be made for this problem to occur less frequently.
- Look at your family tree (see page 15) and see whether this problem has come up before – maybe in another generation.
- Consider how you may have helped perpetuate the problem.

**Changing the script**
- Don't expect someone else to change first: you have to take the initiative.
- Don't see yourself solely as a victim of circumstance: you have to take some responsibility for your family life and relationships.
- Share any observations or discoveries you have made with the appropriate person(s).
- Decide what positive action you can take. For example:
  - take a bird's eye view (see page 11)
  - say what you mean
  - create or respect appropriate boundaries
  - don't scapegoat or form malignant alliances.
- Pay attention to how, when and where you say/do things.

---

found out who is who in the plot. You have learned about common family routines and ways in which you can get more control over them. You have also discovered ways of changing familiar lines. Now you can try to put it all together.

## FORECASTING FAMILY CRISES

Family life goes through distinct phases, with many predictable crises. Knowing about these makes it possible to anticipate some of what is to come and write the new script(s) accordingly. By rehearsing alternative strategies or taking evasive action one can avoid some of these typical family crises, or at least lessen their impact. Being prepared for some of the trials and tribulations of, say, adolescence, courtship or divorce, will help the family move reasonably smoothly from one phase to the next in its never-ending cycle.

Unlike an individual's life cycle, which starts with birth and ends with death, the family life cycle has no clear beginning or end because there is always more than one person involved. When the first baby is born to a couple, for example, the issues for the new parents are quite different from those facing first-time grandparents. In another family, a young person leaving home may coincide with the death of a grandparent and the retirement of a parent. This is why the life cycle of the family is best represented as a spiral. As the younger family members move along the inside of the spiral, the older individuals find themselves moving gradually towards the outside, on their way to late adulthood and, eventually, death.

Different cultures put special emphasis on specific life cycle transitions. Jewish families mark the transition from boyhood to manhood with the significant ceremony of *Bar Mitzvah*. Many black American families place particular importance on funerals, probably as a result of centuries of suffering, and death is therefore seen as a great liberator, taking the suppressed to a happier after-life. Unlike other cultures, the last thing average traditional Italian families want is for their offspring to leave home in their late teens or early twenties; instead they prefer to integrate their children's spouses into

**Family life cycle**

their ever-growing families. Immigrant families therefore frequently encounter problems during their children's adolescence when the teenagers are exposed to very different cultural norms and expectations at school.

It's seldom easy for anyone to adapt to new situations. The very idea of change can trigger a crisis, with feelings alternating between excitement and panic, optimism and pessimism. Change presents a potential threat to any family's equilibrium. Everyone has to face the challenge of playing a different role or coping with a change of set. Moreover, from time to time, we have to adjust to the entrance or exit of a new or old member of the cast. If one is unprepared or under-rehearsed it will take a long time to grow into the new role, with a lot of boos and hisses on the way.

Making the change from one phase to another is always difficult – and families and their individual members are vulnerable during the transition period. In the face of a new situation some behave as if nothing had changed. For instance, there are parents whose children left home years ago who continue to run their houses as if this had never happened. Each 'child' still has their own room even though it has not been used for decades. The parents are totally preoccupied with their children's welfare – as if they were still toddlers. Endless telephone calls, constant invitations, never-ending advice – all this may keep the 'children', often in their thirties, psychologically dependent. In fact, when they do come home they may start behaving like toddlers.

Most families resist change and some members will be keener on keeping things the same than others. This creates an imbalance. Yet, for growth to take place, the family and its members need to deal with each life cycle phase in a satisfactory way. If they don't they pay a price. The chart on page 69 describes the different phases most families go through, the tasks they are likely to encounter, the changes they may have to make – and some of the most common problems encountered in each phase.

The next few chapters describe the different stages in the family life cycle and some of the most common problems which arise. As the various phases overlap, and many events occur simultaneously in the different generations of any given family, we could start almost anywhere. We could begin with the birth of a baby, but this is preceded by two people getting together – two people who, not so long ago, were children themselves...

## FAMILY LIFE CYCLE STAGES AND PROBLEMS

| PHASE | TASK | REQUIRED FAMILY CHANGES | COMMON PROBLEMS |
|---|---|---|---|
| becoming a couple | commitment to one another and each other's families of origin | agreeing roles and goals, negotiating sexual relationship, realigning relationships with extended family and friends, establishing mutually satisfying relationship | sexual problems, infertility, headaches, back or chest pains, anxiety states |
| becoming parents | integrating new member | adjusting twosome to threesome, negotiating parental roles: wife, woman or mother? Husband or dad? Restricting social life, realigning relationships with grandparents | crying, feeding and sleeping problems, 'baby blues', marital tension and affairs, child neglect/abuse |
| growing children | nurturing | balancing home and outside world (school), practising separation | 'out of control' child, bedwetting and soiling, tics, jealousy and fighting, school problems, abdominal pain/headaches, parental communication problems |
| adolescence | establishing new boundaries | balancing control vs independence, permitting to move in and out of family, encouraging 'otherness' and experimentation | staying out late and running away, domestic violence, school refusal, truancy, eating disorders, sexual problems, parental headaches |
| the family in mid-life | leaving/letting go | parents start 'new' relationship, filling the 'empty nest', independence for home-leaver, different child/parent relationship | 'mad' or eccentric behaviour of young person, marital discord, mid-life crisis, inappropriate partnerships |
| the family in later life | coping with loss and changing roles | dealing with illness and death of (grand)parents, coping with grandchildren, dealing with loss of job and friends, adjusting to widowhood | bereavement and prolonged grief reaction, depression, dementia, physical illness |

*Chapter 4*

# Getting coupled – romance and partnership

IN THIS CHAPTER WE LOOK AT:
•
WHAT ATTRACTS PEOPLE TO ONE ANOTHER
•
HOW PARTNERSHIPS ARE FORMED
•
COPING WITH MARRIED LIFE
•
COMMON RELATIONSHIP PROBLEMS AND
SOLUTIONS

At some stage in their lives most people long to share their thoughts and feelings with someone special outside the family, and may dream about falling in love and achieving the perfect union. Celebrated in literature and song throughout the ages, love and romance are central to many people's lives. How well – or badly – we deal with love can have a major impact on us. Love can be a force for good or a force for evil; it can keep us sane or drive us mad. And it often does not last. In fact, we fall *out* of love as fast as we fall *in* love.

In Western societies there are no longer any hard and fast rules about how to meet potential partners, what to do during courtship, and when or whether to get married. Gone are the days when society or the family had a major say in who went out with whom. Arranged marriages are a thing of the past, and factors like property and class have become less important. In recent years homosexual relationships have become more acceptable; so much so that in some countries it is now possible to get married to a partner of the same sex, although this is not to say that one no longer encounters discrimination against lesbians and gay men. Inter-racial and cross-cultural marriages are now relatively common, despite the fact that racial prejudice continues to exist.

Whatever one's cultural origins or sexual orientation, getting coupled is usually full of drama and excitement, the most important thing in both partners' lives at the time. In this chapter we look at the three distinct stages: falling for someone, committing oneself and settling down.

## ACT 1: ROMANCE OR HOW WE FALL FOR ONE ANOTHER

When boy meets girl – or is it the other way round? – anything can happen. And it is no different when girl meets girl or boy meets boy. But why do we get infatuated with a particular person? Partner choice is the result of many different factors and nobody can claim to understand fully why Jack falls for Jill, Jane for Judy or Jack for John. After all, we have it on good authority that 'love is blind'.

There are, of course, many seemingly simple explanations for why we get infatuated with another person, ranging from 'her eyes' or 'his professional success' to 'I felt lonely' or 'she seduced me'. Physical and material factors can play as much of a role as temperament and 'chemistry'. Lust at first sight may be a major reason why we initially feel attracted to another person. No doubt it can subsequently turn into love – but often it doesn't. Some one-night-stands – with hardly a word exchanged – have to do with a whole range of emotions: passion, resentment, boredom, loneliness, disappointment, anger and so on.

One may make a conscious decision never to stick to a

partner for longer than twenty-four hours because one wants to remain independent or not be distracted from pursuing one's career. But there is usually more to it than that. Our actions are only partly driven by reason; we are also subject to irrational forces and these are tied up with past experiences and expectations which we are often less conscious of. For example, seeing our parents struggle all through their married life in an appalling relationship can make us sceptical about committing ourselves to a similar ordeal. Or, having been brought up by 'remote control' through a series of nannies or childminders, we may never have formed a strong attachment to one significant person and therefore have difficulty in doing so with a partner. And then there are those individuals who are extremely close to one of their parents which can make it very difficult to create space for another person.

Whatever the conscious reasons for our infatuation, our family background affects whether and how we form relationships. If we do not want to avoid partnership altogether then, consciously or unconsciously, we tend to look for partners who will help us deal with issues that we have not been able to deal with in our family of origin. We hope that, with the 'right' partner, we will feel safe and loved. Thus when we fall for someone we can be totally convinced that this person is 'right' for us even though it may be obvious to everyone else that we have made a bad choice.

*Marianne, the youngest of five children by ten years, was more or less brought up by her older sisters. Her birth had not been planned and happened despite her mother having been sterilized. Marianne was now in her twenties and, as far as her family, parents and sisters were concerned, she always seemed to fall for the wrong person.*

*Although she came from a respectable background, she usually went for men who had been in prison, mental hospital or both. Nobody in the family could explain why she was fatally attracted to these men who would inevitably get her into trouble. She kept forging cheques to pay their bills, shoplifted on their behalf, and nursed them when they were recovering from their alcoholic binges.*

*None of the relationships lasted more than a few months and they would all end with her partners dropping her. She would then feel miserable and be comforted by her parents who would also say 'We told you so.' Days later Marianne would embark on a similar relationship, with equally disastrous results.*

Why do so many of us, like Marianne, keep getting it wrong? Surely there are a number of reasons. And to know which applies in any one case, one would need to know more details. However this should not stop us thinking about why some 'Mr Rights' and 'Ms Perfects' are the opposite of what we are consciously looking for. For example, in Marianne's case, falling for unsuitable men means that she is never too far away from the bosom of her family. As the relationships are short-lived she temporarily breaks away from her parents, whilst staying in sight. Her parents cannot help but worry about their 'child' even though she is now in her twenties. Marianne perhaps feels that she now gets the parental love and concern that she may have missed out on as a child.

She will know that her birth was not planned and that, prior to her arrival, her mother and father had intended to retire permanently from their job as parents. So, knowingly or unknowingly, she engineers situations whereby her parents' anxiety is increased so much that they became very involved. This involvement may also be partly because they feel guilty about having neglected her in the past. Some parents resent having to return to the task of parenting at a fairly advanced age: others indirectly welcome it, as it gives them a job, perhaps at a time when they have retired from work and have a lot of spare energy.

### 'Right' and 'wrong' partners

*'Why, when I wanted the opposite of my dad, did I end up with a carbon copy?'*
*'How, when my ideal woman is my mum, do I manage to go for girls who are entirely different?'*

Falling in love with another person is a very personal affair – or so most people think. As we have seen, however, it does not happen in a vacuum; it is deeply connected with past experiences and current family dynamics. Some young people like to please their parents and therefore choose partners who seem 'right' as far as their parents are concerned. Yet a partner who may be reassuring for the family can be extremely unexciting for the young person. Conversely, plenty of partner choices are totally wrong in the parents' eyes and therefore 'right' as far as the young person is concerned because they help him or her to separate from the family. And, to complicate matters further, a person who seems like the right partner at the courtship stage may be quite wrong a few years later.

*When Bill, aged twenty-one, moved in with Jack, Bill's parents were utterly horrified. As far as they were concerned it was bad enough that Bill had the 'wrong' sexual orientation, but to live with a man as old as his father seemed too much. All links were severed between the parents and Bill for a few years. Whilst this was very painful to Bill initially, it helped him find out who he was – away from the intense pressure to conform to family values and ideals.*

*When Bill's relationship with Jack came to an end he lived
with a male partner his own age. He then made contact with his
parents and, having gained a sense of security about his
lifestyle, he was able to tolerate their different views without
feeling personally disqualified.*

Some partner choices clearly serve particular functions: for
instance to make a statement to one's family that one has
different values and ambitions from theirs. To suggest, however, that partner choice is entirely to do with pleasing or
antagonizing one's parents, would be far too simplistic. Yet
most young people cannot help being affected by what their
parents (and brothers and sisters) think about their choice of a
partner – even if only to oppose it.

## Why opposites often attract

When looking at certain couples we are often puzzled as to why
people who so obviously come from very different backgrounds
or who have such apparently incompatible outlooks should
want to be together. The conventional wisdom that 'opposites
attract' doesn't seem to explain it. Natural curiosity and the
erotic excitement one can derive from being with someone
entirely different may be some of the reasons. But the novelty
can wear off fairly quickly. Perhaps other factors are at work?

*There were many reasons why Jackie hated her father. He had
always put her down and ordered her around as if she were his
servant. Much to her surprise, Jackie (tall, good-looking and
physically very much resembling her father) developed a taste for
short, fat, ugly men. Without exception, these partners would
put her on a pedestal and when they started criticizing her, she
dropped them. She often laughed when she told her friends
about her latest conquest who, in their eyes, seemed identical in
all but name to the previous one. Jackie's friends thought it very
peculiar that she kept falling for people who were so different
from what they regarded as her 'ideal' man.*

When we have been seriously hurt or abused by a parent, we
may have a strong wish to hitch up with someone who repre-

DIY EXERCISE: RELATIVE RELATIONSHIP RATINGS

Here is an opportunity to compare your relationship with the one your parents had.

• First, rate the quality of your parents' (and/or step-parents') relationship on a scale from 1 to 10 (1 being rock bottom and 10 representing sheer ecstasy) under the following categories:
  – relaxing together
  – showing physical affection
  – sexual relationship
  – emotional closeness
  – not keeping secrets from each other
  – talking to each other
  – mutual understanding
  – helping one another
  – dealing with money matters together
  – taking care of one another.

Don't worry if you don't know the details of your parents' relationship. You are allowed to guess.

• Add up the total score (top marks would be 100), and decide whether you think this adequately represents the quality of their relationship. Make adjustments if necessary.

• Now do the same for your own relationship and, if you wish, get your partner to do the same.

• How do the scores and scripts differ?
  – Has your relationship scored more or less than your parents'?
  – Look at the scores for each category: are you replicating their script?
  – Does your partner agree with you on the scoring? How does s/he see it differently?

sents a lifestyle as different as possible – preferably in a country some 10 000 miles away. Characteristically in such cases the chosen partner will be totally unlike one's own opposite sex parent. Why? Because a daughter, like Jackie, for instance, may loathe her father so much that she cannot bear the thought of her lover resembling her father in any way. She will therefore stop herself from falling for someone who may even have only very superficial similarities, fearing that this might result in an identical relationship to the one she had with her father.

Can one do anything about this? It depends whether the person herself regards it as a problem. For all we know, Jackie (or whoever) may feel all right about leading her life in this way. However, if she is perturbed by her actions and feels out of control, she may want some help. Making connections with past experiences can then help her to see her partner choice in context and understand why she finds it impossible to stay in love. Maybe she needs to test whether all men who resemble her father also behave in identical ways. Based on new experiences, she can then revise her assumptions.

**Going for more of the same**

Many people stick with the familiar and go for a person with similar family background, similar profession, similar friends, similar everything. Occasionally they go as far as trying to find a person with a similar nose: familiarity is reassuring, but at the same time breeds contempt if not boredom.

At different times in their lives people may have quite different needs. At one point in one's development peace and a 'safe' person may be all that is required. Replicating the script of the parental relationship can be reassuring: following the proven family recipe, passed down from generation to generation, is bound to work, and will also please the parents.

If we feel we had a good deal from our parents we may look for a partner who is similar to the one our (same sex) parent chose. For women this traditionally means a male partner who resembles Father, and for men a wife who seems like Mother. Whilst it may be reassuring to follow familiar recipes, in reality it is rather difficult to find the perfect substitute for Mum or Dad. And discovering this may be a slow and painful process.

ACT 2: FORMING A PARTNERSHIP

When two people get together they carry 'baggage' from their pasts – to do with their families of origin and other important sources. This baggage consists of anything from assumptions about gender roles or general ideas about 'appropriate' ways of having or avoiding sex, to specific rules about tidiness or diets. Such baggage can weigh any couple down. It can get in the way of forming a partnership which is about what to drop, what to keep and what to take on in the present (which friends to drop, what paper to read, how to load the dishwasher, when to have sex, and so on).

A partnership involves the joining of two people of the same or opposite sex and their respective family and friendship systems. This is bound to be a highly complex process as it means examining and discarding some of the baggage from the past. The initial stages of forming a partnership, once both people have decided to share the same flat or house, can be turbulent. This often manifests itself in apparently ridiculous battles about how to decorate and arrange the joint living space.

*As a child Jenny had always wanted to paint her bedroom pink. Her parents simply would not permit this – they wanted it to be, as they put it, 'white and clean'. Jenny could not wait to have her own place and when she set up home with her boyfriend, Jeremy, she insisted on painting every room pink. Initially he did not mind, but after a few months it started irritating him intensely.*

*When his male friends made fun of him for living in a pink world, he told Jenny that he wanted the sitting room painted light blue. After much discussion Jenny agreed. When Jeremy wanted to change the colour of the hall, Jenny protested. A few weeks later another room had turned blue and after another month only the bedroom remained pink, her partner's concession to her childhood dreams . . .*

Living together means negotiating the concrete details of everyday life and many relationship battles are fought indirectly, using paint, furniture or pictures on the walls. How people succeed in transforming their living space into their joint home often reflects the balance of the relationship. There are houses which bear all the signs of stuck negotiations, with

DIY EXERCISE: WHOSE PLACE IS IT ANYWAY?

- Look at your flat or house – whose stamp do you detect? Is it shared or is it more yours or your partner's? Do you feel you live in someone else's space?
- Examine each of the following rooms: bedroom, sitting room, kitchen, bathroom. Look out for the following signs:
  - colour scheme
  - ornaments
  - plants
  - furniture
  - position of furniture and other objects.
- Make a rough estimate of how much is your planning and how much is your partner's.
- Consider how you would change things if it was totally your place. What would you remove? What might you add?
- Imagine what your partner would do if s/he had a free hand . . .
- If you want to make a lot of changes you probably do not feel very much at home. Now consider the pros and cons of discussing this with your partner . . .
- What would you have to do for you to feel it was a bit more yours? Identify one or two specific steps. Consider discussing these with your partner.
- Has s/he come to the same conclusions? If not, why not? Discuss the implications of change.

no paint on the walls, or, another extreme, half a room painted pink and the other half blue . . . There are places where he has 'his' room and she has 'her' room. Unable to arrive at a mutually satisfactory compromise, some couples take decades to convert their flats or houses, with the majority of rooms left as unfinished as their negotiations.

When she moves into 'his' place she may never feel at home; certainly not as long as they both continue to behave as if it was 'his' place. If the partners cannot find a way of making it *their* joint place then this usually produces problems. 'His' place may be inhabited by a 'ghost', perhaps that of a previous partner who has imposed her personal stamp and tastes. These reminders of the past can haunt the new relationship, but initially may not get talked about.

Very occasionally it suits both parties not to question the idea that it is 'his' and not 'theirs'. It allows the 'lodger' to feel relatively uncommitted and the 'owner' can remain wedded to his precious possessions without the fear of giving anything up. Whilst such arrangements can last for a while, there usually comes a point when 'she' eventually gets fed up with living out of boxes. It is only when she one day unpacks their contents, thereby obstructing vital parts of his elaborate stereo system, that the long overdue confrontation takes place. But is it necessary to wait that long?

### Why kitchen sink issues can be so annoying

Forming a partnership also means sorting out apparently trivial kitchen sink issues. Who does the washing up and when, who writes the shopping list, who is in charge of the cooking, who takes out the rubbish – all this involves establishing routines. After some heated arguments over breadcrumbs on the floor or the size of cucumber pieces, partners often step back, laughing in disbelief at how they could possibly have allowed themselves to get so steamed up about 'nothing'. In many cases the kitchen can become a major battleground, where the ground rules for the relationship are fought out. Cooking and cleaning soon reveal people's notions about what's right and what's wrong, and also about who is more right. Most couples eventually find their own idiosyncratic solutions, ranging from strict 50/50 arrangements to clearly divided roles of 'cook' and 'dishwasher', or utterly chaotic arrangements involving take-away meals and part-time cleaners – until the funds run out. If no solution is found, the battles can spread into areas other than the kitchen.

Television is a major trouble spot for many couples. If partners have different interests there is plenty of scope for arguing about whose turn it is to choose which programme. Solutions range from strict turn-taking to the purchase of a second TV set. The latter course of action avoids conflict but has the disadvantage of not helping partners learn how to compromise.

Another common battle between new partners is over how loud the music should be. 'Turn it down' usually elicits the answer 'But then I can't hear it.' These and many other issues require the development of negotiating skills. When these fail we find a young couple sitting in different rooms plugged into their respective electronic equipment, only having the occasional fleeting encounter by the fridge while replenishing their supply of comfort food or drink.

The other major areas for couples to negotiate over are money and sex. It is a fact of life that two people do not necessarily feel desire at the same time. The ensuing discussions are often painful. 'Don't you find me attractive any more?' is the common question, begging the answer 'Of course I do.' Lack of desire might be blamed on a headache or stress at work. Jealous speculation leads to indignant denials and hollow protestations of 'undying love'. Unfortunately many partners find it too difficult to create time and space to discuss their sexual relationship frankly. Instead, they hide their embarrassment or disappointment behind mutual accusations.

At times the only way forward is to seek professional advice, such as marriage guidance counselling or couple therapy. Here the presence of a third person provides an opportunity for each partner to listen to the other, something that might be unthinkable at home where they are much more likely to shout and scream or walk out on each other. The counsellor or therapist will not only try to enable both partners to hear one another but also make suggestions as to how to experiment with something new or different so that some novelty can be introduced into the relationship.

'Romance without finance is a nuisance' was a popular 1930s song. Money has broken many hearts and relationships. When two people decide to set up home together they need to make decisions about whose money it is – his, hers or theirs? Some couples budget and others live from day to day – in hope. Thankfully, the traditional pattern of the male partner handing out money when his wife begs for it is less common than it was. But shared bank accounts have their pros and cons: on the one hand they are a statement about the couple's new status of togetherness. On the other hand, this can be at the expense of independence when one of the partners uses it to monitor the other's financial 'performance' or spending decisions.

When couples eventually sit down to discuss money matters, it can be helpful for both partners to draw up a list of spending and saving priorities. If this is done separately then each partner has the chance to reflect on his or her priorities and notes can subsequently be compared. There may turn out to be a surprising amount of agreement and this will result in decisions that both partners can back.

**Learning to share and compromise**
Becoming a couple means arriving at a consensus over many issues, something perhaps never previously learned with one's brothers or sisters. The apparently trivial arguments people have over decor, cooking and TV programmes relate to the deeper issue of how the couple is going to get (it) together. Both partners need to give way to some extent.

Relationships where this does not happen have a tendency to go sour eventually, with one party becoming increasingly

DIY EXERCISE: DEVIL'S ADVOCATE

This technique can be used in order to help reach a compromise between partners.
• Decide which issue you need to compromise on.
• Each write a separate list of priorities.
• Hand your list to your partner and take his or hers.
• Argue in favour of each point on your partner's list, giving reasons why your partner's priorities might be correct.
• Listen while your partner does the same with your list.
• Put both lists down and be silent for 5 minutes: think about the similarities and differences between the two lists.
• Take back your own list and see whether you can incorporate any of your partner's points. Try to rewrite it, changing at least one point. Ask your partner to do the same.
• Now compare notes: any chance of a compromise?

aggrieved. Close relationships are characterized by both partners sharing major parts of themselves without being afraid, thereby revealing their strong as well as vulnerable sides. This implies not censoring one's thoughts or feelings, and trusting each other.

People who have had healthy attachments in their families of origin find it easier to trust a partner. Healthy relationships tend to be characterized by a mutuality of wishes and fears. If something goes wrong, both partners take responsibility, rather than one blaming the other.

**More unfinished business**
The process of negotiating the banal issues of everyday life is not without pain. Having specific expectations can put enormous strain on the other partner: if one does not come up to scratch, one feels unloved, unsafe and lost. As we have seen, most people tend to experiment with relationship patterns based on earlier experiences in their families of origin. For example, when a man brought up by his depressive mother

DIY EXERCISE: STOPPING PHYSICAL VIOLENCE

If you are violent to your partner:
• Recall the last episode of violence
  – what was it that made you see 'red'?
  – how did things escalate?
  – how and when could you have stopped this escalation?
• Identify issues or situations that have in the past resulted in you being violent
  – which of these are still around and likely to recur?
• Consider how and whether these issues can be resolved or defused
  – by calm discussions, compromise or avoidance?
• Remember that only *you* carry full responsibility for hitting your partner – no matter how much you feel 'provoked'
• Make things safe for your partner. Think how to take evasive action next time round:
  – go for a walk, invest in a punchbag, scream under a railway arch or move out and away.

If you are at the receiving end of your partner's violence:
• Examine the first three points above:
  – last episode of violence, trigger factors and avoidance or defusion tactics.
• Predict the next likely episode and make a detailed plan of what you are going to do so that you don't get hurt.
• Be clear about the warning signs and consider the various options to keep yourself (and children) safe, like:
  – not participating in the escalation
  – physically removing yourself and/or permanent separation
  – finding a women's refuge.
• Don't take responsibility for the perpetrator's violence, but take responsibility for your own safety – do not rely on the violent person's promises that he'll never do it again
Note: If you are involved in a violent relationship then you are both in desperate need of help. It can be dangerous to experiment with self-help strategies, such as the ones listed above, and you may well require professional assistance (see addresses page 219).

lives with a woman who is also depressive, he may – without realizing it – have become stuck with what is familiar.

> *Mona, a woman in her thirties, physically maltreated as a child by her father, teamed up with an apparently kind man who, after a honeymoon phase, turned out to be a wife-beater. She said that being maltreated by her partner was the last thing she ever wanted, but she could not leave him. When she eventually did leave him she fled into two further violent relationships.*

Are the majority of men wife-beaters, then? Or was Mona, perhaps without realizing it, seeking out a dreaded though familiar scenario? Many abused women find themselves in abusive relationships with men, possibly through an unconscious wish to re-experience an old scenario in the hope of handling it better than when they were helpless little children. Many may feel that one way of dealing with unfinished business is to keep seeking out similar scenarios until one feels that one can walk out on the person one chose – something that one never thought possible as a child.

The fact that there *are* a few women who repeatedly get involved in violent relationships of course in no way absolves the wife-beater from having to take full responsibility for his violent acts, rather than seeing himself simply as the victim of his wife's (alleged) nagging. Unfortunately many men (and also a few women) try to justify spouse violence by claiming that they were 'driven' to it. It is possible that a person who is used to being beaten by her partner may know exactly what to do or say to provoke him. Whilst this in no way excuses his violent behaviour, it perhaps makes it more predictable – the next time round.

## ACT 3 SETTLING DOWN: MARRIAGE AND OTHER FORMALITIES

Once the initial hurdles of forming a partnership have been overcome, it may be time to settle down. For many couples it becomes important to formalize the relationship, not least because there may be tremendous pressure from the family.

This seems somewhat odd these days, as most men and women have sex before marriage, and many partners live together before getting married or have had a succession of lovers before eventually committing themselves.

Whilst it was once thought only natural to marry, it is no longer considered essential. Engagement and marriage can still, however, provide a show of strength and loyalty, sending a message to the world at large and the family in particular. For some people, deciding whether or not to marry can have a remarkably unsettling effect, as it threatens to spoil a previously romantic and carefree relationship. The mere prospect of marriage can result in one or both partners suddenly getting cold feet. People are often surprised to find that, having cohabited happily for many years, an impending wedding can fundamentally alter the balance of their relationship. This is not surprising: there is the fear of being trapped, ambivalence about committing oneself, and lingering doubts about one's partner.

### Commitments and what they stir up

*Rita and Alan had been, in the words of both their families, 'living in sin' for three years. When they decided to get engaged, and set a date for the wedding a year later, there was a sigh of relief from the prospective in-laws. But not from the young couple.*

*Alan wondered aloud whether or not he was 'ready to commit myself for life' and Rita felt upset that he should think of marriage as a prison. This made her question whether he really wanted to get married. She packed her bags, moved out of their flat and called the wedding off. This desperately upset Alan who begged her to return. He involved her family who he knew were very fond of him.*

*When he told Rita that he had changed his mind and that he was now 'eighty per cent certain' he wanted to marry her, she became even more enraged. Despite her own family's considerable pressure to return to Alan so that he could make an 'honest woman' out of her, Rita decided to remain independent.*

What do we mean when we say that someone is 'not yet ready' for marriage? Commitment has something to do with loyalties.

These can lie with your family of origin or with your identity as a single person. Setting a wedding date or taking out a joint mortgage raises the issue of commitment and fears of being trapped. Some people are literally not ready to leave the bosom of their own families or believe they have not had their freedom – yet. Individuals who 'fell' into a relationship the moment they left home often feel that they haven't really tasted independence yet, and are reluctant to cement their relationship through marriage. 'I shouldn't have married so young . . .' is the regretful refrain of those who feel that they have missed out on something.

Bowing to pressure from others surely is not the best reason for getting married and committing oneself 'for life'. What does 'being ready' involve? Firstly, it is important that both partners feel, more or less, equally ready – otherwise there is an imbalance from the start.

Assuming your partner feels ready, are *you* ready to commit yourself? To answer this question you may wish to list some of the things you feel you could no longer do if you were married. These are most likely to involve one or more of the following: money, sex, friends, hobbies, work, travel, family. Now consider how you would feel if you gave your partner up. Would the other 'things' be worth it?

**Marriage across barriers**
Whereas many families seem to tolerate their offspring having casual relationships with partners from different ethnic, religious or class backgrounds, when such relationships threaten to become permanent all hell can break loose. For a good Jewish boy to marry a non-Jewish girl can be a disaster in the eyes of his family. When a white woman marries a black man, previously covert racism can burst out into the open. And there are those 'nice' English families for whom nothing could be more horrific than to be presented with a 'bloody foreigner' as the prospective son-in-law.

This begs the question: why do these people pick someone they know their family won't approve of? Is it pure love or is it a conscious or unconscious attempt to shock their parents? If it is the latter it may be an important way of giving the parents a message but does not bode well for the future success of the relationship, thereby ironically proving the parents right in the end. Often it is not easy to separate one's motivations. Very few young people freely admit to themselves or others that their partner choice is based on wanting to annoy their parents. Whatever the underlying causes, the net result is often that hypocrisy is exposed, class prejudice comes to the surface, and the 'child' risks being emotionally and/or morally disowned.

The wedding can end up being a highly dramatic event with plenty of intrigue beforehand. Who should attend? And if there are different religions, which one is to be used for the ceremony? If the immediate family is excluded, what effect this will have on them? And who will be blamed for it?

*Carl and Jessica decided to get married in style. Jessica had been conceived during an affair her mother had had with a foreigner whilst she was married to the man Jessica had assumed was her father. The secret was revealed during her late teens and some twenty years later she managed to track her natural father down and had occasional contact with him. Her mother had not seen her ex-lover since before Jessica's birth. But Jessica wanted her father to attend the wedding and her mother, somewhat anxiously, agreed.*

*Carl's parents, on the other hand, had divorced and remarried other partners some twenty years ago. His mother had left his father for another man whom Carl had come to know and love as his step-father. His own father, however, although allegedly happily married, had never forgiven his ex-wife for leaving him and had refused ever to meet the man she left him for. He refused to come to the wedding, as he did not wish to meet his ex-wife's not-so-new husband.*

*When Jessica discussed this with her family, her step-father suddenly announced that he himself did not want to attend the wedding if Jessica's natural father came. As if he had heard this, the natural father telephoned the following day from abroad, saying that his wife was very much against him coming to the wedding as she had hoped that his affair with Jessica's mother had long since been forgotten . . . In the event Jessica and Carl decided to ban all family members from their wedding.*

Many couples have to find a way of dealing with such pressures and either decide to have a minimalist wedding or risk old family feuds erupting whilst the wedding cake is being cut.

### Keeping it all in the family

One of the greatest challenges facing a newly married couple is to define their relationship with their families of origin. This is easier said than done. Whilst many couples struggle for years to get the balance right, for others it may be highly desirable to become part of a large family.

Some people get married because they want to enter someone else's family, perhaps the sort of family they never had themselves and always yearned for. Such a match is perfect if the chosen partner is happy to remain 'married' to his or her own family. This sort of arrangement may suit everybody, and in some Eastern societies it is quite common. Even though it may not be everyone's idea of normal family life in Western culture, it only becomes a problem if one or more members are unhappy about it.

*Peter came from an unhappy family where his parents cared very little for him. Jackie was ten years younger when they married. She was the youngest of three children and the older boys had left home in their late teens. Jackie had remained the loyal daughter. She and her retired parents went everywhere together: shopping, holidays, cinema, even sports. The parents' friends were Jackie's friends and Jackie's friends quickly became the parents' friends.*

*Jackie met Peter when she was twenty-six and he was her first boyfriend. The family immediately 'adopted' him and he welcomed this as he no longer had any contact with his own parents. He spent every night at the family's house and when their engagement was announced everyone was overjoyed.*

*The couple even invited Jackie's parents to join them on their honeymoon. It was a happy occasion, but soon afterwards Jackie developed severe back pain. This required her to stay in her parents' house, as they were able to look after her whilst Peter was out at work. As their house was big enough they invited Peter to live there permanently. When the couple announced*

*that they had decided not to have children 'for some time'
because of Jackie's back problem, everybody 'understood'.*

*Medical advice was sought for the back problem, but none of
the specialists could find anything physically wrong. Jackie
refused to see a psychiatrist as she and her family were
convinced that there was nothing psychologically wrong with
her. In fact, everybody pointed out that she was very happy
'despite her disability'.*

This is an extreme example of how certain arrangements,
however odd they may seem to outsiders, can suit everybody. In
this case the price paid for the family's excessive closeness was
back pain. This symptom allowed Jackie to stay in the family
whilst at the same time fulfilling the family expectation to get
married. In some families there are unwritten rules that women
have to get married, otherwise they are 'failures'. What better
solution than marrying a 'tame' husband, someone who was
prepared to fit into the family? In this way Jackie could fulfil
family expectations whilst remaining at home. This situation
can suit certain men, particularly those who have no contact
with their own families: here then is an instant family with
caring parents, the sort these men may never have had.

So, what about the back pain? Jackie and her husband
indirectly told the family that it stopped them from having a
sexual relationship. (Sexuality and children would have given
them a separate identity as a couple.) As it was, Jackie's minor
back problem turned out to be a convenient symptom which, if
focused on, maintained the status quo: a happy family with a
married daughter in the home. This family found a 'solution'
which seemed to satisfy everybody – for the time being.

This phenomenon explains why some physical symptoms
seem so hard to cure. At a later stage, when Jackie and Peter are
ready to be a couple, a minor bone manipulation or massage
may be the catalyst for change. What about helping Jackie
now? Paradoxically, but understandably, the Jackies – or Peters
– of this world would often rather remain stuck with their back
pains or families, until they feel ready to let go of them.

Whilst this is an extreme example, many of us may participate in more minor forms of the same scenario. We will feel

---

DIY EXERCISE: CHART YOUR EMOTIONAL DISTANCE

This little exercise may help you assess how strongly you and your partner are connected with your respective families of origin. Collect monthly scores for each of the following:

|  | Partner A | Partner B |
|---|---|---|
| • How many visits? Who visits whom? | | |
| • How many telephone calls? Who calls whom? | | |
| • How much money lent or given? By whom to whom? | | |
| • How much advice? From whom to whom? | | |
| • How many incidents of interference? From whom to whom? | | |
| • How many hours spent on thinking about family? | | |

Now compare your findings with those of your partner and discuss with him/her whether they are surprising and need to be changed.

---

loyal to our families of origin, particularly if we had an enjoyable childhood. We may then dream, from time to time, of all living happily together in a large extended family. Whilst we would probably wish to be less tied down than Jackie and Peter, we would nevertheless keep up contact with our families. The telephone is one means of maintaining such contact and there are many families in which the married woman rings her mother every day for at least an hour, and then calls her sisters to discuss what their mother has said.

Financial dependence can make it difficult to 'cut the umbilical cord'. Wealthy in-laws can be a blessing but also a curse:

---

DIY EXERCISE: CUTTING THE CORD

---

If you feel that you or your partner are too closely connected to your/their parents:
- Share your concerns with your partner.
- Discuss with your partner whether contact and dependence can or should be reduced.
- Agree on what the ideal arrangement should be, and think about the first small step you could take towards that goal, e.g. reduce telephone calls and/or visits, not accept money, not inform them of your every movement or plan.
- Try to predict the family's response.
- Work out how you are both going to handle their response, e.g. give in totally, compromise, or remain firm.
- Plan what the next few (small) steps might be.
- Predict the family's responses and work out how you are going to handle them.
- Set yourselves a realistic time limit in which to achieve your desired level of independence.

Note: Both partners need to agree on the strategy and be equally willing to implement it.

---

He: *'If we didn't have my parents we'd be lost.'*
She: *'If your parents hadn't always given you money, you'd have a job by now.'*
He: *'But they don't mind supporting us . . . it gives them a purpose in life, it makes them feel useful.'*
She: *'But they destroy us in the process.'*

Having your in-laws as part of your marriage can be very uncomfortable. Indeed, it may eventually cause so much tension that you are forced to choose between giving up money or giving up your relationship.

Partner choice is often largely influenced by both families of origin, with each family hoping that their offspring's chosen partner will strengthen existing family ties. Most people, however, eventually outgrow their families. Sometimes this process can be speeded up through one's partner. If he is not liked he can become a wedge between his wife and her parents, knowingly or unknowingly altering the relationship between her and the various members of her family.

This may be a convenient way of separating from one's family of origin as the 'evil husband' can be blamed, thereby excusing the wife as the victim of his 'unreasonable' wish to cut the family cord. If she lets her husband fight the battle with her family, she becomes the innocent bystander and the son-in-law is singled out for blame.

This is one way of resisting the almost magnetic pull exerted by some families. However not many sons or daughters-in-law like to become defined as a wedge and this can be avoided if the partner shoulders some of the responsibility for keeping a distance.

### Living in Mother's shadow

When a man accuses his wife of being insensitive and keeps telling her that his own mother would have been much more understanding his wife is likely to say that she is sick and tired of always being compared with his mother. The more he tells her how much better his mother was at cooking, serving meals, making beds, etc, the more irate his wife will get. When she eventually asks why he did not marry his mother in the first place, he will probably accuse her of being jealous. She is then likely to reply that she is pleased not to be anything like his mother, and this will be greeted by the husband as proof that his wife hates his mother.

In this case the husband is using his mother as a weapon against his wife in order to disqualify her possibly valid criticisms of him ('My mother would have been more understanding'). If she has any doubts about her own abilities this strategy is likely to succeed. People with plenty of self-confidence will be almost immune to such manoeuvres.

Ironically, it is often those men who feel that their mothers did not care for them well enough who attempt to cope with this disappointment by idealizing them. What better way is there to put Mother on a pedestal than to form a partnership with a woman who does not (want to) 'come up to scratch'?

Seeing his wife fail makes his mother's shortcomings seem less severe. The good son (and bad husband) can rest secure in the knowledge that all women are more or less hopeless, with his mother being the least bad of the bunch! The past looks positively rosy compared with the daily reality of what he perceives to be his nagging wife. Moreover, by behaving in this way he can avoid criticizing his mother directly, as his wife is doing that job for him. His wife has, without realizing it, become his mouthpiece.

To be on the receiving end of this sort of warped comparison for prolonged periods can be very frustrating. And the more the man praises his mother, the more his wife is likely to rubbish her. One way of breaking the deadlock is for the woman to adopt the praiser's position – even if this is very hard. Pointing out her mother-in-law's strengths rather than her weaknesses and defending her actions changes the dance. There may be suspicion but no disagreement and, possibly, the loyal son may eventually start voicing his own criticisms of his mother.

Incidentally, this 'mother-in-law problem' is a very (stereo-)typical scenario. Similar ones, involving husbands and fathers, are equally common.

## ACT 4: THE CHANGING PARTNERSHIP

*Once upon a time she was twenty and he was forty. She was what he called 'young and inexperienced' and she thought he was 'wise and helpful'. He had two failed marriages and three children. She had just lost both her parents. He was a lecturer and she was his student. She passed her exams at about the same time as she passed the test to become his wife. She looked up to him and did what he wanted. He looked down and after her, particularly when she was ill. They often told one another how well matched they were.*

Sometimes we choose people who we, arrogantly, perceive as 'inferior'. Professor Higgins in Shaw's *Pygmalion* certainly derived a lot of self-worth from this. Choosing a partner who is 'non-threatening' rather than 'exciting' may be reassuring for a time – until everyday boredom sets in and one starts fantasizing about a more adventurous partner.

> *Twenty years passed. She was now forty and he was sixty. She had become what he labelled 'feminist and militant' and he was now what she described as 'the perfect example of a male chauvinist'. They now had two children at university and one child still at school. She had a good full-time job. He had just accepted a voluntary redundancy package. She was radiant. He was depressed. The more radiant she became, the more depressed he got. She liked looking after him when he was depressed. When he stopped being depressed he became unbearably demanding.*

Relationships are rarely stagnant – they change over time. If only one person changes, the other will be left behind. This creates an imbalance and if it is not dealt with it can rock the marital boat. Teacher–pupil relationships, though common, rarely work in the long run. Most students graduate and all teachers eventually have to retire.

## Stale and stereotypical marriages

After the initial adjustments and negotiations it is not uncommon for couples to put their relationship on 'automatic pilot' for many years. This may be convenient, as each partner is now more than familiar with the daily routines. The family machinery continues to run smoothly, with the occasional bit of fine-tuning.

It is only when partners feel that they are being controlled by the relationship, rather than being in charge of it, that established roles become less acceptable. Though this may be obvious to outsiders, it is not always apparent to the people inside the relationship.

A vague feeling that all is not right may eventually lead one partner to start questioning whether their respective roles have perhaps become stale or stereotyped. Overleaf, then, is a little exercise to determine whether you are in such a stereotypical relationship.

What may be a boringly stereotypical relationship or

---

DIY EXERCISE: DO YOU HAVE A STEREOTYPICAL MARRIAGE?

- Tick how you run your marriage:

| | Man | Woman |
|---|---|---|
| – Who carries the rubbish out? | | |
| – Who does the ironing? | | |
| – Who does most of the cooking? | | |
| – Who cleans the toilet? | | |
| – Who clears the drains? | | |
| – Who is more likely to have a headache when you want to have sex? | | |
| – Who most often refers to their own mother as an example of how things should be done? | | |
| – Who has most control over the money? | | |
| – Who changes the light bulbs and fuses? | | |
| – Who is better at driving? | | |
| – Who is usually right? | | |
| – Whose decisions are usually implemented? | | |

- Now tick how your partner may have answered these questions. How do you explain the differences (if any)?
- Decide whether your marriage is stereotypical. If it is, do you mind?
- Consider what would happen if you changed a few of your traditional roles or tasks.
- Discuss this with your partner. You could experiment with just reversing the roles every other day – so you don't change things too radically.

Be warned: changing familiar roles too drastically and too quickly can destabilize relationships!

marriage to one couple may be bliss to another. Gender- and role-stereotypes exist in abundance in our society and some of us choose to be more politically correct than others. In some cases political correctness can start to become a paralyzing stereotype in itself.

## Chapter 5

# From twosome to threesome – the first child

IN THIS CHAPTER WE LOOK AT:
•
**HOW AND WHY COUPLES DECIDE TO
HAVE A BABY**
•
**PREGNANCY AND ITS EFFECTS ON THE
RELATIONSHIP**
•
**THE IMPACT OF THE BIRTH**
•
**BABY BLUES AND LEFT-OUT FATHERS**
•
**HOW YOUNG FAMILIES ADJUST**

Napoleon Bonaparte remarked towards the end of his life that 'it is horrible to see oneself die without children'. Many people feel that it is important to procreate; to pass on their genes, traditions and good (or bad) advice. Wanting to see aspects of oneself replicated in another person may seem somewhat self-indulgent. But there is more to it than that.

DIY EXERCISE: CONSIDERING THE PROS AND CONS OF
HAVING A BABY

Here are some questions that partners can ask themselves and
each other to clarify the effects of having or not having a
baby. (Some of the issues will be different for partners with
different cultural backgrounds and for gay or lesbian couples.
For instance their decision may be influenced by exposure to
racial and sexual discrimination.)

• What will happen to our relationship if we do not have
  children?
  – List all the positive things
  – List all the negative things.
• What will happen to our relationship if we do have children?
  – List all the positive things
  – List all the negative things.
• What are the advantages and disadvantages of having a
  pregnancy now?
  – List the advantages
  – List the disadvantages.
• What would be better/worse if it happened in twelve
  months' time?
  – List the advantages
  – List the disadvantages.
• How would things be now if there were children around?
• How will prejudice and discrimination affect our
  relationship and the child's happiness?

Note:
Each partner can answer these questions individually and
then compare notes. Alternatively, the couple can try to
answer them together. If the exercise is done separately,
considerable differences may be revealed which could lead to
a fruitful though possibly heated discussion.

P.S.
• If you are still undecided, would you leave it to fate? Why?
  – List the advantages
  – List the disadvantages.
• What would you do if there was an accidental pregnancy?

## DECIDING TO HAVE A BABY

Many couples see parenthood as the blessing of their union – a tangible sign of their love. For such parents, the urge to procreate involves the desire to replicate their partner as much, if not more, than to replicate themselves. Wanting to care for somebody else is a fairly universal urge, and many people have a natural curiosity about life and how it develops. Having a child is a way of understanding this mystery and giving a purpose to one's life.

However there are many other reasons why couples decide on a pregnancy, some of them conscious, some less so. These may include: finding a 'job' and providing a goal in life; making a statement to others and/or oneself about being 'grown up'; wanting to give a child the love one did not experience oneself; cementing a relationship, with the baby as 'super-glue'; providing a 'gift' for one's own parents (the prospective grandparents).

Whatever your reasons for having babies, rational thought is

only part of the equation; and the same is true when deciding against babies. Plenty of couples come up with very convincing arguments as to why it is cruel to bring a child into 'a world like this . . .' with references to pollution, the disappearing ozone layer, wars and food shortages. Who could argue with that? And who would disagree with the view that the last thing a bad relationship needs is a baby?!

Less obvious reasons for deciding against a pregnancy include: fear of commitment; bad experiences as a child in one's family of origin; fear of not being a good parent.

Whatever the final decision, most couples (including many gay and lesbian partnerships) do consider the pros and cons of having a baby. It is only natural to be in (at least) two minds about such a major decision. The arrival of a baby is likely to change life considerably and affect the partners' relationship.

**The baby as growth experience**

Some people decide on a pregnancy merely because they are bored. A baby seems to offer a sense of purpose in an otherwise empty life. This may appear to be a bad reason for having a baby, but there are plenty of 'aimless' mothers or fathers who do find their true vocation in life through parenting. Linked with this may be a desire for clear adult status. Young people may consider having a pregnancy because they want to feel grown up and able to make their own life and death decisions.

*One of the things Bunny and Sean had in common was that they were both the youngest children in their families. Bunny was never taken seriously by her parents and was constantly teased by her older brothers and sisters. She had never been any good at anything and her self-confidence was at an all-time low when she met Sean.*

*Bunny was only sixteen at the time and she fell for Sean because he seemed just as shy and lacking in confidence as she was. Sean was as young as Bunny and when she started talking to him she discovered that nobody believed in him and that he felt very belittled by everyone. After a few weeks they decided to have a baby and proudly announced this to their parents and extended family. This news was greeted with*

*disbelief and ridicule. Bunny and Sean were now more*
*determined than ever to prove that they could do it.*

Having a baby early can also be linked with wanting to get away
from school and further education. It can fill a gap. It can be a
statement to yourself and your parents that there is something
good about you. And, in many cases, parental opposition is
likely to strengthen the teenager's wish to go ahead with becoming pregnant.

### The baby as compensation

Without perhaps being conscious of it, the motive for having
babies can be the wish to look after someone else in a way one
never experienced oneself. A person might want to demonstrate to their parents that they made a mess of it and show how
much better a parent he or she can be. Proving this to the
parents can become quite a crusade, with the baby's own needs
sometimes coming second.

*Peter, the middle child, always felt left out. He believed that his*
*parents were more interested in his two sisters and from the age*
*of twelve he thought a lot about how much better a parent he*
*would be, once he was old enough. His parents tried to explain*
*to him that they loved him as much as their other two children,*
*but Peter was determined to do a better job than them. He had*
*set his mind on having three children and treating them all*
*equally well, particularly the middle child. He could not wait for*
*this to happen, and proposed marriage to several young girls.*
*   He was only sixteen when he got his first girlfriend pregnant*
*and by the age of twenty he was the proud father of three*
*children. His parents were surprised at what a dedicated parent*
*he was and could not fault him on anything. Peter never*
*stopped reminding them of their own shortcomings and how, in*
*his view, they had spoilt the youngest. He made sure that this*
*was not repeated in his new family until his wife expressed her*
*concern at how neglectful she felt he was with their youngest.*

Wanting to compensate for real or imagined 'sins' of the past
can lead to a strong urge to become a parent as soon as

possible. But once the baby is born, young people soon realize that parenting is not such an easy job after all. A new appreciation of one's parents' struggles can follow, putting it all in perspective.

### The baby as adhesive

When relationships go wrong both partners start to think about possible solutions. At times having a baby seems the ideal way to regain the closeness they have lost. Some of these couples do acknowledge that this may be unfair on the baby, but in the face of impending break-up people are rarely rational. Pregnancy is used to patch up the relationship, in the hope of a better life in the future. The baby, before it can even speak, is meant to glue it all together – what a responsibility!

Why do people do this? Is it fear of loneliness or maybe a belief, nourished by years of parental brainwashing, that having a family should be their major goal in life. We frequently hear about the woman who tries to trap a man into a permanent relationship by becoming pregnant. But there are also

---

DIY EXERCISE: THE PUPPY TEST

---

Pets can be very testing. Taking on a puppy is a full-time job and faces the owners with some of the pleasures and strains that are in store for parents: from feeding to training; from cleaning up to sleepless nights . . . Thinking about buying a puppy and how to look after it may be a good preparation for 'the real thing'.

- Discuss with your partner:
  - whether to buy a puppy
  - if so, what kind and what age
  - when would be the best time
  - who would look after it
  - who would feed it
  - who would take it for walks
  - who would look after it when you're out at work
  - how this would affect your holiday plans
  - how it would affect your social life.
- Now decide whether or not you are going to invest in a puppy.
- Multiply all the pleasures and stresses you anticipate by 100 to predict your responses to having a baby!

---

plenty of men whose only hope of keeping their lover is to cooperate in producing the baby she desperately wants. He is not particularly interested in the baby but will 'put up with it' to be with her. However, using a pregnancy to cement an unstable relationship rarely turns out to be a good long-term strategy.

**The baby as gift to the elders**
Some parents cannot wait to become grandparents, and their wish to have a grandchild can put enormous pressure on a young couple who may, eventually, oblige by 'giving' a baby to their own parents. This may help the grandparents avoid facing the prospect of losing their own grown-up child. Replacing a child with a grandchild is a common scenario in

families. Leaving home but filling the empty nest with a new 'chick' keeps up links and preoccupies the grandparents with more part-time parenting tasks. The baby is a 'gift' to the grandparents and weaves new webs of dependence.

> *Dorothy was seventeen when she had Jane. Much of the parenting was left to Dorothy's mother, as Dorothy was regarded as being too young to look after her own daughter properly. A generation later, when Jane announced at sixteen that she wanted to have a baby, Dorothy, to Jane's surprise, was very enthusiastic. It appeared that she was very much looking forward to a second chance of parenting: this seemed like a good opportunity to 'get it right' second time round.*

A daughter's loyalty to her own mother is one thing. But where does this leave the prospective father? Does he have any say in how the child is parented? If the couple have little chance to discuss and decide for themselves what they want, this is rarely a good start. Old business interferes with a newly-forming family, leading to the child growing up with two mothers, Mum and Granny, and plenty of room for confusion and rivalry.

Family pressure can work both ways: some people give in to it, while others fight it and do precisely the opposite of what is expected. Families can exert subtle and not-so-subtle pressures on their offspring which can be extremely annoying, particularly when they start invoking family traditions.

'We have always', 'Surely you agree that you should' or 'in our family it is normal' are some typical opening lines when family traditions are being quoted. These include:
- If the couple do not conceive within one year of marriage then there is something wrong
- Children are the fulfilment of any woman's ambitions
- Grandmothers need to teach young mothers how to handle babies
- Everyone deserves grandchildren.

**The baby as life sentence**
As we have seen, the reasons for having a baby are rarely clear-cut. The same applies to the reasons against. A child entirely

changes the life of the couple and many people are daunted by the prospect. For them it may seem like a life sentence – a narrowing rather than a widening of horizons. Those of us who are afraid of entering into long-term commitments had better think again. It is worth bearing in mind, however, that it is often a question of timing: what may seem a life sentence at one point may feel much less threatening at another stage.

Hidden behind a fear of committing oneself may be the fear of not being a good parent. Although this may sometimes be irrational, it is frequently based on past experience – both good and bad.

*George had always admired his parents. They seemed so balanced, had always been available for their three children, and had helped to turn each of them into happy and successful individuals. Moreover, their own relationship was a very happy one, with few conflicts and hardly any arguments.*

*George found it difficult to leave home at the age of twenty-five when he started living with his first serious partner. Over the following decade he had a number of relationships with different women, but felt that none promised the sort of perfect marriage his parents had had.*

> *All seemed different when he finally settled down with Cora –*
> *until they discussed having children. George became preoccupied*
> *with his potential inadequacies as a father. He could not help*
> *comparing himself with his father and his and Cora's*
> *relationship with that of his parents. He felt he could never be*
> *as good a father as his own dad had been . . .*

Idealizing one's parents and then comparing oneself with
them can be dangerous. Thankfully, perfect parents do not
exist and near-perfect parents usually give their offspring
enough confidence to consider themselves potentially good
parents. How, then, do parents end up being idealized by their

---

DIY EXERCISE: CONNECTING PAST AND FUTURE

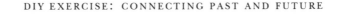

**Step 1**
- Draw up a balance sheet of your parents' behaviour towards
  you as a child – with positive aspects on the left and negative
  ones on the right. (You may want to differentiate, if
  appropriate, between your father's or mother's parenting.)

| What parents were good at | What they weren't good at |
|---|---|
|  |  |

(e.g. playing, listening, being truthful, hugging, taking you
  out, comforting you, telling stories, reading to you, inviting
  your friends over, cooking your favourite dishes, etc)

**Step 2**
- Now study this list. Is it evenly balanced? Are there too many
  good or too many bad aspects?
- Looking at the *negative* side of the balance sheet, ask
  yourself some of the following questions:
  - Assuming that my parent(s) wanted to be really good at
    parenting, how come they didn't manage all that well?
  - What stopped them? Was it their upbringing? Their
    relationship? Other pressures?

offspring? Such parents may love and respect each other so much that they never quarrel or criticize one another and may require their children to be equally uncritical.

If the children grow up in an environment of such unqualified mutual admiration, they will not only keep things to themselves but will also stop themselves having bad thoughts about their parents. Their thinking thus becomes internally censored, with the parents being placed on pedestals that could be cracked if they ever thought about them in a critical fashion. By keeping your parents on a pedestal you compare yourself unfavourably with them, particularly when contemplating whether or not to become a parent yourself.

---

- What is similar about my/our current situation?
- What is different?
- Which of the above are likely to be repeated if I become a parent myself?
- What can I/we do to stop this happening? Or is it inevitable? What have I learned from my parents' experiences?
- Looking at the *positive* side of the balance sheet, ask yourself some of the following questions:
  - What made it possible for my parent(s) to do this so well?
  - How likely is it that I/we are going to be as successful?
  - What in my/our current situation might stop us being so successful?

**Step 3**
- Now draw up your own balance sheet of what you think you might be good or bad at if you became a parent.
- Look at how much overlap there is between your balance sheet and that of your parent(s).
- Now test your notion that your parents were much better/worse at parenting than you could ever be. Ask yourself why you shouldn't/couldn't be a different parent from those you had.
- Discuss your findings with your partner.

---

Idealizing one's parents is one extreme, demonizing them is another. Bad memories of one's childhood and the fears of turning out to be as bad a parent as one's father or mother are not uncommon. But why does history necessarily have to repeat itself?

*Josie was fifteen when her mother committed suicide, leaving her in charge of her two younger siblings. Josie's grandparents put them up in their large house, but Josie remained her two brothers' 'little mum' – as they affectionately called her. There was little contact with their father who had left the family home years earlier for another woman. Josie had nothing but contempt for her father and she continued to idealize her mother despite what had happened.*

*She never talked about her mother's suicide or expressed any feelings about having been let down by her. At the same time she took a very grim view of family life and she would never consider becoming a parent herself. Josie felt she had done part of her parents' job in bringing up her younger siblings and subsequently missed out on her adolescence. She had a series of partners, but having a baby was never on the agenda.*

*It was only when she was thirty-seven, the age that her mother had died, that she became restless and depressed. First she was puzzled by these feelings and then realized that it was somehow connected with her mother's life and death. She established contact with her father whom she had refused to see for nearly twenty years.*

*Josie was now interested to find out more about her parents and she started seeing them both in a different light. Making sense of her history brought her closer to her father. It also helped her face up to her strong feeling of being let down by her mother as well as remembering many of her good points. Ten months later Josie, who had been living with a steady partner for five years, became pregnant and was looking forward to becoming a mother.*

When people are stuck with viewing their parents as all good or all bad this paralyses them so that they cannot make any decisions about whether or not to become parents themselves.

At this point it may be worth re-examining the past, although doing this can open up old wounds. Removing an idealized parent from their pedestal or finding something good in a horrible parent can be painful, but it may help the person move forward and enable them to make decisions about their own lives.

## PREGNANCY AND ITS EFFECTS ON THE RELATIONSHIP

When the couple finally decide to have a baby and when Mother Nature has obliged, then a new phase in their joint life unfolds. How couples react to pregnancies varies a great deal. With some, nothing much seems to be different – apart from the bump getting visibly bigger. They almost seem to have forgotten what is going to happen. At the other extreme we have the 'pregnant couple', totally preoccupied with each second of the foetus's development, obsessed with health and the right foods, exposing the unborn to certain pieces of music, and talking to it at night. For them the baby is a living person long before it is born.

The majority of couples fall somewhere between the two extremes. The growing foetus is a reality to them; they listen from time to time to its heartbeat, feel its shape and slowly start preparing the nest. Some pregnancies go smoothly but many do not. Either way, they can strain the relationship.

**Female and male fads**
Pregnant women are known to have the most unusual fads, from a sudden desire for Brussels sprouts and bacon at 3am to a seemingly unlimited appetite for treacle tarts. Such fads are concrete signs of changes taking place, some of which are triggered at a hormonal level. These desires can be very intense and the partner's reluctance to go in search of the required item can be interpreted as his lack of commitment to being a father . . . Being understanding, sympathetic and obliging is the only way of dealing successfully with these seemingly irrational food crises, however late at night they occur!

But men also have their midnight fads and these usually come down to one extremely basic need: sex. As the foetus grows, some men become very sensitive, if not jealous, and may make increasing demands on the mother-to-be. If she doesn't feel like having sex this can lead to the accusation that 'the baby is more important than me', a taste of what is to come once the baby is born.

Pregnancy can be a trying time for both partners, as new needs arise and old ones cannot be adequately satisfied. Many couples find ways of making allowances. Others become increasingly frustrated, as neither partner feels that their needs are being met. Unfortunately this rarely gets brought out into the open. Discussing these changes is usually crucial.

**Preparing the nest – or not**
Preparing for the new arrival is important for most couples. Changing the colour scheme of the room, buying baby equipment and clothing are only a few concrete examples. They represent the expectant parents' acknowledgement that a new person is going to enter their lives and that this requires them to create the necessary emotional and physical space for it. When couples actually start making these preparations varies and can reflect the extent to which one or both partners are preoccupied with becoming parents. At times it is the well-meaning grandparents who force the pace . . .

*Tracy and Lee were both in their late teens. It was Tracy's first pregnancy and they were both very much looking forward to having a baby. In the later stages of the pregnancy they made many expeditions to the city centre looking at cots, baby baths, changing tables, prams and other baby equipment. Doing this gave them pleasure, and discussing the relative merits of one cot over another was their way of thinking about life once the baby had arrived. They took a long time to make decisions and felt fine about this.*

*Tracy's parents, however, saw this as a lack of maturity and felt they should speed up the process. One day a big van arrived, loaded with all the latest equipment ready for an instant baby room. Much to the parents' surprise the young couple were not*

DIY EXERCISE: GUESS WHAT YOUR PREGNANT PARTNER
WANTS FROM YOU

Most of us are pretty good at making our own needs known to
our partners. We are less competent at guessing what they
want from us. This exercise can be done by both the pregnant
woman and her partner at the same time but on separate
pieces of paper.

• Draw up a list of your partner's new needs, brought on by
  pregnancy, e.g.
  – s/he wants more sex
  – s/he wants to be left alone
  – s/he feels too pampered and wants less attention
  – she wants to be made to feel good about her changing
    body
  – she wants to be more protected
  – s/he wants more time together
  – s/he wants to think about preparing the nest.
• Show your list to your partner and find out whether your
  partner agrees with your assessment of his/her new needs.
• Pick one need each, and think how to fulfil it during the rest
  of the pregnancy.

*grateful but angry: they sold it all within a week and gradually
replaced it with items of their choice. The parents were hurt, but
the young couple had made their first big statement about being
a new family, with their own likes and dislikes.*

Single mothers – having been let down by the father of the
child or deliberately excluding him from the pregnancy –
often have a much harder time preparing for the birth. They
may need to rely on family support to make the necessary
preparations. If the expectant mother lives with her parents
she may have to put up with their good or bad advice, possibly
reviving old memories of being treated like a child by her
parents, or causing her to develop new dependencies. It can,
however, be a very positive experience. Mother and daughter

may connect in new ways, the experience of parenthood bringing them closer together, as they compare notes and discuss past issues in a new light.

Despite much current political propaganda against one-parent families, there is little evidence to suggest that they are necessarily more likely to have problems because there is 'only' one parent. There are plenty of cultures where children are born into extended families, with multiple care-takers, with good results. In our so-called advanced Western societies the isolation and low social status of single parents may well be major causes of many of their problems. The disappearance of the extended family has certainly made the task of being a single parent more difficult. And if our society gave more support to single parents we would probably focus more on the problems of two-parent families.

There are many reasons why parents have difficulties with preparing the nest and end up leaving it to the last moment. Take the teenage mother who tries to conceal her pregnancy from her parents. Entirely unaware of their daughter's changing shape, her parents are thrown into being grandparents, literally overnight.

Living in an environment where the very idea of a teenage pregnancy is unthinkable, the young girl will have found it impossible to plan ahead to the time when she is to become a mother. Like her parents, she will try to deny that she is pregnant, hiding the growing bump under loose clothes. Under these circumstances the baby only becomes a reality the day it is born, with the family in a major crisis, hovering between acceptance and rejection.

With young parents it is not only the mother and father who need the nine months of preparation but also their immediate families, as they may be called upon to help. Denial of the pregnancy by the expectant mother and the larger family is rarely a good start.

Apart from concealing a pregnancy, due to unbearable family pressure or the expectant mother's mixed feelings about having a baby, there can be other reasons for reluctance to prepare the nest. Although perhaps obvious to outsiders, these are often not apparent to the couple. For example, families who have experienced a series of miscarriages or stillbirths may develop a tradition of waiting until the baby is born before rejoicing. Terrible disappointment in the past is bound to lead to caution, if not a belief that one may not be capable of producing a living baby.

This may not be based on the direct experience of either partner but some unspoken fear that dictates their behaviour. Sometimes one hears references to not 'tempting fate' by buying the cot before the baby is born. In such cases it is important to explore these underlying fears and face rather than deny them so that the baby can become a reality before it is born, allowing the couple to plan ahead and make some of the necessary adjustments.

There are many specific issues that arise for couples who adopt a baby and only a few can be mentioned here. Prospective adoptive parents have usually gone through many hoops to prove that they want to have a baby and that they are capable of providing it with a good home. The vetting process may have taken a long time, with hopes being raised and dashed in quick succession.

Adoptive parents can be 'on call' for years and it is very difficult for them to know when or whether to prepare the space for a new arrival. There is no nine months' warning. Instead, a suitable baby may suddenly turn up, requiring the couple to make major rearrangements in their lives and work, often from one day to the next. This can put severe strain on the relationship, though most adoptive parents cope with this very well as they have been desperate for a baby for years.

### Parental fears

Fear of losing the unborn baby is fairly universal. Many expectant parents are very careful during their first pregnancy and the pregnant woman's partner is likely to behave very protectively. He may go as far as telling her what to eat or how to live more healthily, and this often leads to arguments. At one level there may be some justification for remarks such as: 'If there is something wrong with the baby I am going to blame you . . . You don't look after yourself.' However these comments usually fail to take into account the expectant mother's own deep-seated anxieties, including her changing appearance.

Parental anxieties can often be linked with past personal or family experiences. As we have already seen, in a family with a record of miscarriages the pregnant woman may start expecting history to repeat itself. If she herself was born after a series of miscarriages or a stillborn child this may lead her to think about why she survived and her siblings did not. If she does not talk about this to her partner, he will be puzzled by her sadness and perhaps even angry that she is down at a time when she should be happy.

Other expectant parents may find that their feelings become increasingly mixed as the pregnancy progresses. Not looking after oneself may be an expression of not caring about having a baby. Drinking and smoking excessively may be the woman's way of, perhaps unconsciously, getting rid of the baby. Often this sets up tensions between the partners, as he may be more protective and try to nag her to live more healthily. Conversely, if he has second thoughts, he may, consciously or unconsciously, neglect his partner or start 'accidentally' bumping into her abdomen.

**Terminating pregnancies**
Couples often discuss what they might do if they find that the woman is carrying a malformed or handicapped child. These days the ready availability of antenatal tests creates anxieties as well as allaying fears. However, on the whole, couples seem to fare better if they are able to talk in advance about whether or not they would want to go ahead with a termination, should the test results indicate a high chance of having a handicapped baby. Religious beliefs, family pressures and social circumstances are some of the major issues likely to influence their decision which will always be a difficult one.

There are many other issues that couples struggle with. For example, having wanted a baby for years, suddenly the timing may seem wrong if it conflicts with work interests or one partner's priorities at the time.

*Sarah, thirty-eight, had been living with Nick for eight years. He had two adolescent daughters from his first marriage who lived with the couple. They had often discussed having a child of their own, but the timing never seemed right. There were plenty of tensions in the home and having a baby, with all its demands, seemed like asking for trouble. At the point when both daughters left home Sarah suddenly fell pregnant, something she had longed to be for quite some time.*

*When she found out, she told Nick but his unenthusiastic response filled her with doubts about whether the timing was indeed right. As he saw it, for the first time in twenty years he was without any direct obligations towards children and he wanted some 'freedom'. Sarah felt torn and then decided to have a termination, intending to have a baby in a few years' time.*

*Initially she felt relieved, but some months later, around the time the baby would have been born, she became very weepy. Nobody understood why she felt so low. After all, her job was going well, and her relationship with Nick seemed to be thriving. Sarah herself could not make the connection with her hidden grief over losing the baby. Nick was no help, as he felt they should 'get on with life – we can always have a baby later'.*

Two partners' differing needs may lead to a compromise which suits one more than the other. In life-changing situations, such as deciding whether or not to have a baby, the after-effects are often under-estimated. Anniversaries, such as the day the baby might have been born had it not been aborted, or a year after the termination, can become important landmarks. Some would-be parents become intensely preoccupied with the life they might have been leading if the child had lived. Men tend to be much less affected by these issues and may therefore see their partners as 'hyper-sensitive', haunted by the ghost of a baby that never was. Such bereavements may require outside help as well as an understanding partner.

## BIRTH, AFTER-BIRTH AND EARLY DAYS

The arrival of a baby is a major event. No amount of foresight can prepare the couple for the changes that are about to transform their lives. It is a major transition: the partners are no longer just partners but also parents. Most couples feel worried and confused, if not totally lost, when first holding their tiny offspring. There is so much to adjust to – how to feed the baby, when to sleep, and what to do in which order.

But what is often most stressful is the impact of conflicting needs and demands: the combination of a screaming baby, an exhausted mother and a frustrated father can be overwhelming. When you add to this the demands of the wider family to see and hold the baby, invading the house at odd hours and drinking to the baby's health – you have a situation in which even the most competent new parents fear for their sanity.

What, then, are these conflicting needs? The baby's needs are for food, warmth, baths, nappies, sleep and stimulation. Mothers need peace, comfort, sleep, love, space and much else besides. Fathers need to feel included and involved, have a role, be looked after (a bit) and get some rest. Then there are their needs as a couple – time for one another, talking, intimacy, fun . . . The new family also needs some time to be a threesome, with some boundaries around them and not too much disturbance from the outside. Then there are the members of the extended family who need to feel helpful, who want to give advice and make it easier for the couple.

It is clearly impossible to respond to all these different demands adequately and this inevitably causes tensions. One partner may accuse the other of being 'inconsiderate' or the grandparents may call the parents who ask for some peace and quiet 'selfish'. Inevitably someone will feel left out. Many couples dance around the baby so much that they ignore some of their own vital needs, such as peace and space. This may not show in the initial euphoria but signs of distress may develop soon after.

Some of this distress can be averted if both parents can be honest about their own needs and tell each other when things get too much or when they need a break. Being appreciative of one's partner is also particularly important at this time.

### From baby blues to post-natal depression

When mothers feel low in the days following delivery we talk about the 'baby blues'. In fact their moods swing up and down,

---

DIY EXERCISE: FEELING BLUE?

---

**Spotting the signs**
– loss of appetite
– marked exhaustion
– sleeping difficulties
– irritability
– weepiness
– self-denigration
– listlessness
– loss of confidence
– low self-esteem
– intermittent feelings of despair
– lack of interest in the baby
– blaming the baby.

**What partners, parents or friends can do**
– Do not say 'pull yourself together'
– Make positive rather than critical remarks
– Don't allow her to bottle up strong feelings or thoughts
– Get her to talk about how she feels, and listen!
– Help her to organize pleasurable activities with the baby
– Give her some space for herself by providing regular 'time off' from the baby
– Think of how to break daily routines
– Encourage her to take up an activity that has given her pleasure in the past
– Arrange a night off for the couple
– Help her to make contact with other mothers
– Encourage close friendships.

---

from euphoric highs to tearful lows, but they usually settle down after a few days. About two-thirds of mothers are affected by the baby blues which are linked with the dramatic hormonal changes that follow giving birth.

A more worrying condition is post-natal depression which affects up to 30 per cent of mothers. Hormones or other chemical imbalances are often blamed for the depression but this is usually only part of the story. One of the major factors is lack of confidence: doubts about her capacity to be a good mother or to breastfeed properly; worries about her changed body or her ability to be a good partner. Another factor is lack of support: an absent or unhelpful spouse; uninterested parents; lack of friends with whom to share her new concerns; financial strain; loneliness.

As there is an expectation in our Western societies that the woman should be the main nurturer of babies, any discomfort displayed by the child can be interpreted by the mother as a failure in her parenting. This may well be linked with old unresolved feelings about the way one was parented oneself. Questions about the past get raised. Was I looked after well by my mother? Did she feed me properly?

This feeling of incompetence can turn to anger which a parent may sometimes be tempted to take out on the baby. A screaming baby is a test for any parent and being cross with the baby for apparently never being satisfied is a natural response. Some parents feel they are not good enough and get temporarily cross with the baby for facing them with their shortcomings. They feel as if the screaming baby is being ungrateful for all the love they have given. Exhaustion sets in and it becomes easier to lose control. Lashing out at a screaming baby can be the result and is a typical symptom of post-natal depression.

However post-natal depression rarely happens suddenly, and spotting the danger signals can help to prevent it turning into a major problem for everyone.

**Left-out fathers**
Since men have generally been trained not to be weepy, it is more difficult to spot signs of the 'paternal blues'. Fathers tend to throw themselves into their work, stay out late and go to the pub to relive the good old days with long-forgotten mates. Angry outbursts are common. Fathers frequently see themselves as victims of the new love affair between mother and baby and rarely ask how they may have contributed to their own predicament. The breast-feeding mother can make the father feel that there is nothing useful he can do at this stage because she possesses all the goodness the baby needs. When

he voices this, she may feel pressurized into choosing between feeding her baby or her partner's ego.

How can this sorry state of affairs be avoided? Fathers need to have a role from the very start. Nature has disadvantaged them by not allowing them to get pregnant and they therefore have a lot of catching up to do. The more they are given to do, the more involved they become and the less left out they feel. Men, like women, need space and a network of friends with whom to share some of their concerns. More than women, they need to be encouraged to talk about what's happening, with their partners and friends.

### Changing nappies and roles

The seemingly endless cycle of crying, eating, pooing and sleeping can be very exhausting. However much one has read on the subject, the arrival of the first baby is a huge step into the unknown. It is only normal to turn to someone for advice. However, putting oneself in the position of asking for help may in turn reinforce one's feeling of helplessness. Some people not only turn to books, but bring up their children entirely by the book. There is a danger that one will start believing in other people's home truths rather than one's own. If there are too many experts, how do you learn to trust yourself?

*Mary left home at the age of eighteen to live with Rob, very much against her parents' advice. They predicted that the relationship would not last but three happy years later Rob and Mary had a baby. Mary turned to her mother for advice the minute their little daughter was born. The proud granny spent every day from early morning to late evening in Rob and Mary's flat 'helping Mary with the baby', as she put it. Mary and her mother experienced a closeness they had not had since Mary's early childhood. Looking at the baby they would reminisce about those days.*

*Rob soon started to feel pushed out. He was not allowed to handle the baby, as Granny always seemed to know best. He soon spent more and more time away from Mary and the baby and eventually moved back to live with his mother. Mary now relied entirely on her own mother who she felt was so much more competent. She moved back home with the baby, as she felt she could not cope on her own. Her mother was very happy to look after them both.*

Young parents lose confidence in their own ability to parent if they do not give themselves a chance to learn how to cope with the baby's daily demands. Only if they experiment will they find their own solutions. Over-keen grandparents and other unhelpful 'helpers' can perhaps initially make a useful contribution. However, if they stay they cause problems for the couple: too much help makes people feel helpless.

## Chapter 6

# Taming monsters – families with young children

IN THIS CHAPTER WE LOOK AT:
•
CHILD AND PARENT TEMPER TANTRUMS
•
WHY CHILDREN MISBEHAVE
•
REWARDS AND PUNISHMENTS
•
WHY CHILDREN REGRESS
•
SIBLING RIVALRIES AND SELF-FULFILLING PROPHECIES

## THE TERRIBLE TWOS

As children grow out of babyhood they become both easier and more difficult – easier because they learn to talk and can make themselves understood, but more difficult because they answer back. Despite the development of language many toddlers seem to behave quite incomprehensibly and disruptively: learning to speak has not, apparently, helped them to become more rational. On the contrary, the two- or three-year-old can be overcome by seemingly uncontrollable rages and tantrums which not only tax the patience of the parents but alarm and worry them. Dealing with an explosive and recalcitrant toddler can undermine their confidence in their ability to be good parents and may also severely test relationships within the family.

So, what are the Terrible Twos all about? Are they an inevitable stage in child development? Is there anything parents can do themselves which will make things better – or worse?

The Terrible Twos are an important stage in child development, although not all toddlers succumb to terrifying rages. As a two- or three-year-old the child learns that the whole world does not revolve around him and that it is necessary to develop awareness of others' needs: his parents' need for peace or space, for example. The toddler is also learning that there are rules of conduct to be complied with: for instance, about mealtimes, and that, in some homes at least, ice-cream comes after the main course. And the toddler will be taught about bedtime and how much TV can be watched.

It is only natural that these challenges to the child's sense of self should provoke protest – from 'difficult' behaviour to outright tantrums. Difficult behaviour can easily escalate into tantrums because all toddlers want to test how far they can go. This is not just some kind of perverse naughtiness but an

important way of learning what is acceptable and what is not. All these reactions, from simple 'bolshiness' to outright screaming fits, are very necessary because they help children to realize that their needs can be in conflict with those of others and that negotiation needs to take place. Appropriate parental responses will aid that process, and if they are not forthcoming the child may be at a loss – and eventually need outside help.

It is important to realize that different families have different tolerance levels and therefore assess the same behaviour differently: what amounts to a temper tantrum to some parents is mere contrariness to others. So how should parents react? Whatever one's personal limit is, it helps to remember that this is a phase and that one cannot expect a toddler to have an adult's rationality and self-control. For many parents it is far better, for example, to avoid an escalating confrontation by attempting to distract a child, rather than fighting it out as though dealing with an adult. It is worth remembering that one lesson children learn quickly is that different sorts of behaviour are acceptable in different contexts. For instance, it is easier to be rude at home than in a nursery school where you are expected to behave like a little angel. Children can and must learn to find ways of controlling their frustrations, so there may well be a price to be paid for being over-relaxed about their behaviour within the family.

Surprising though it may seem, most children feel reassured when their parents set limits and show they can cope with their anger. Children want to win and lose at the same time. Defeating their parents and running the show at home, as a little tyrant, is tempting, but being looked after and taken care of is usually even more attractive. Firm and consistent parents, who demonstrate their ability to deal with their toddler's provocations, help them develop into loved and balanced individuals.

If children grow up thinking that nobody can deal with their anger, not even their parents, they start to think that their feelings cannot be controlled. This gives them an inflated sense of power that can be quite scary. Their bad behaviour may then escalate to a point where people outside the family, such as the police, eventually have to set limits – often years later and often too late. In the end it will be reassuring to the child that there is somebody who can contain his or her rage: nothing is more frightening than being out of control.

**Losing your cool**

There comes a point when all the patience and understanding in the world cannot prevent a parent from seeing red. Some parents dread losing control because they know they might shout and scream or even hit their child.

Many people will at times come dangerously close to hurting

---

DIY EXERCISE: KEEPING YOUR COOL

Next time you are worried that you are going to lose your cool with your toddler, try some of the following:

• Weigh up the pros and cons of:
  – ignoring the annoying behaviour
  – correcting it
  – distracting the child
  – promising a reward if the behaviour stops.
• If you are going to do something, do it sooner rather than later.
• If the child has an audience, consider taking him away so that his behaviour does not get reinforced by his peers.
• Focus on the positive: concentrate on something your child is doing well (e.g. 'The picture you drew a few minutes ago was very good' or 'That was a lovely smile').
• If things are very heated, consider:
  – counting aloud up to ten, as a warning to yourself and the child
  – telling the child (and yourself) what is going to happen if s/he does not do what you ask
  – taking some time away from the child (going into another room to cool down or breathing in some fresh air outside).
• Predict when and where similar episodes or crises are going to happen and take evasive action, such as counting up to ten or taking some time out.

---

their children because children do have an unparalleled ability to wind their parents up. Most parents lose their cool with their children on at least one occasion and then feel full of remorse immediately afterwards. Only a few end up causing serious injuries, but it is often difficult to say where smacking stops and hitting starts.

Smacking is meant to be a symbolic act and there are those who believe that 'a good smack never hurt anyone'. Yet there are cases of parents who have seriously injured their children and say in their defence, 'We only smacked him'. Smacking, if it is a controlled action and not an impulsive reaction, deliberately avoiding hurting the child, may be an appropriate way of setting limits for many parents. However, hitting a child, with the aim of inflicting physical pain, can surely never be justified. If it becomes 'common currency' in the home then the older the child gets the harder one needs to hit to hurt. Hurt breeds hurt – where will it all end? Children who get hit have a tendency to hit back. Years later, when they are involved in horrendous fights at school, their parents wonder aloud where they learned it from . . .

## WHY CHILDREN MISBEHAVE

Common sense tells us that children's behaviour is often linked to family dynamics. A child – even a toddler – can spot parental weaknesses and will respond to them. Some children, for example, will consistently stir up trouble by playing one parent off against the other. This is a lesson which no child needs to be taught. And it depends on the parents' responses whether it is discouraged or is allowed to turn into a destructive habit.

*Whenever his dad said, 'No, you can't have a sweet', Leroy, aged three and extremely bright, went to his mum who could not resist his charm. Dad then got cross with Mum who in turn accused him of being too strict. Dad charged her with spoiling their son and she replied that, since he had had a difficult childhood, he was just jealous that Leroy might have a better one. Dad countered by referring to Mum's brother who had been spoilt silly by his mother and 'He's no good now'. Throughout all this, Leroy munched his sweets.*

Why is Leroy manipulating his parents? The obvious answer is so that he can have a sweet. But by doing so he stirs up his parents, and most children do not like to see their parents argue with one another. The parents could see themselves as the victims of Leroy's manipulations and blame him for causing the argument. But in this case they don't. Leroy's behaviour is merely the excuse for them to fight battles, rooted in their own childhood experiences, about whether to spoil children or be tough with them.

Why is Leroy manipulating his parents? The less obvious answer is that the parents welcome and indirectly encourage Leroy's behaviour so that they can use it to make important points about the rights and wrongs of their respective upbringings and perhaps to put each other down. Clearly Leroy does not 'plan' this, but he may have learned that his parents thrive on these arguments.

Some children play one parent off against the other to get their own way, but there are many children whose disruptive behaviour is really a way of seeking to unite their parents. Such misbehaviour is not a conscious activity but something which the child has learned from repeated experience will defuse tension between the parents, even though it results in the child being blamed or hit.

*Rod, Jean and their three-year-old son Terry referred themselves to a child guidance clinic. The parents were in their late twenties and their relationship had always been fairly stormy, with frequent rows, short separations and passionate reunions. Little Terry was not a planned child and by the time he had reached three years of age he had been nicknamed 'Little Terror'.*

*The parents said they could never have a proper discussion, as the little boy would always get between them. This apparently made them both so cross that they felt like hitting him. Instead they shouted and screamed at him all day long and now felt at a loss. In the clinic the parents were asked to discuss a contentious issue. They chose money, which appeared to be a*

DIY EXERCISE: GETTING YOUR ACT TOGETHER

Parents are more effective if they act together
- In a quiet moment decide what particular problem you are going to target. Start off with one problem, rather than two or more.
- Decide what the consequences of the problem behaviour should be.
- Both tell your child what is going to happen next time the problem occurs.
- Try to repeat it a few times, with both of you present.
- Your child will want to test you: both immediately implement what you have decided to do.
- If only one of you is present, remind your child that you have both decided to do it.
- Both let your child know how pleased you are when s/he doesn't repeat the problem behaviour.
- Review your strategy at regular intervals to see if it is working.
- Once the first problem behaviour disappears, tackle the next one – jointly!

Note: the combination of clear goals, parental agreement and consistency will almost always pay off. Single parents can use the same techniques. They have the advantage of not having to argue about what problems to tackle and what consequences to use. But they have the disadvantage of not having a partner as back-up.

*constant source of arguments, and within a few minutes all hell broke loose.*

*At this point Terry, who had been quietly playing with some toys in the corner, got up and started physically getting between the parents. They initially ignored him and continued arguing over his head. Terry then escalated his behaviour, lashing out first at his mum and then at his dad. There was still no direct response from his parents who seemed too engrossed in their argument to notice Terry. When he finally spat at his parents and yelled at the top of his voice, they both screamed at him, picked him up and tried to make him sit down on his chair. Terry fought back and the parents turned to the therapist, shrugging their shoulders and saying, 'See what we've got to put up with?'*

To an onlooker it was fairly obvious that Terry's increasing bad behaviour had the effect of defusing the escalating conflict between his parents. His naughty behaviour stopped the argument and they both united against him.

Children often volunteer to be the 'whipping boy' in an effort to create peace between their warring parents. However, many such scenarios are less dramatic than the one above. Children can become highly attuned to the more subtle cold wars that sometimes exist between their parents. These children realize that the only way their parents can be together is if they have a joint enemy within: in a way they volunteer themselves as scapegoats so that the parental relationship can be maintained. The only thing that unites the parents is their joint concern over the child.

### Reward or punishment?

How and when one rewards or punishes a child is very important. Once again, if parents have not got their act together, the result is likely to be a confused and disobedient child. It is common sense to reward a child for good behaviour and to punish it for bad behaviour. Finding a reasonable balance between the two would seem to be the obvious solution. Yet common sense rarely prevails. Some families, often well-meaning and united, seem to be addicted to negative attention. It is their children's negative behaviour which arouses comment, concern and involvement, rather than their good behaviour, which is simply taken for granted and often goes unnoticed and unrewarded.

Small wonder, then, that the child soon learns that it does not pay to be good. The paradox is that he learns to 'please' by being a problem. Receiving a punishment, or being the focus of negative, critical remarks, is 'better' than getting no attention at all.

---

DIY EXERCISE: KEEPING A PROBLEM DIARY

---

Do you inadvertently give your child more negative than positive feedback? The emphasis can be shifted with the help of a diary. A problem diary focuses on a specific problem, such as temper tantrums, rudeness, not eating, etc.

• First decide which problem you want to observe and over what period of time (e.g. a week or a fortnight).
• Use a piece of paper for each week and divide the space into seven equal parts for the seven days of the week.
• Now make two columns for each day. Record in the first the problem behaviour(s) and what happened, and record in the second column what preceded the bad behaviour, how long it lasted and what stopped it. For example:

| Day | Bad behaviour | Context |
| --- | --- | --- |
| Monday | Turned his bedroom upside down (8am) | Was told to get dressed and go to school. Waited till Dad left for work, then misbehaved. Lasted 25 mins, responded to bribes (sweets). |

• Now select one of the child's good behaviours and do the same on a different piece of paper.
• At the end of the week or fortnight look at both diaries.
• Discuss your findings with your partner or a friend and look for any patterns, such as trigger points, habitual parental responses, which strategies work and which don't.
• Now work out how you can reinforce the good behaviour.

*Craig was only three years old when his mother, a single parent, described him as 'the worst-behaved child that ever lived'. Whatever he touched he would break. He could scream and shout louder than any other toddler and was well known for spitting and fighting. However his mother found it almost impossible to keep a straight face when she discovered Craig's latest misdemeanours. She would tell him off, usually with a big grin on her face. Exhausting though it was, she would spend all day saying 'Don't do that' or 'Stop it' and Craig would take no notice of her whatsoever. On the rare occasions when he was good, his mother would have a well-deserved rest, only to be dragged out of her chair by Craig's renewed mischievous behaviour . . .*

When parents end up only responding to their child's negative behaviour, they may have something invested, often without realizing it, in not clamping down on mischief. Gender-stereotyped views about 'cheeky little boys', for example, perhaps related to some personal experience of, say, a mischievous little brother, indirectly encourage and reward the boy for his 'performance'. Both he and his parent(s) get addicted to this cheeky/naughty interaction – until it gets all too much. The time has come to give the child some praise and attention for good behaviour.

## WHAT IS NORMAL?

The question of normal development has already been touched on in the context of the Terrible Twos, but there are many other stages between babyhood and adolescence which can perplex and worry parents – from potty-training to progress at school.

As we have seen, it is almost impossible and usually unwise to make generalizations: 'normality' is often defined according to long-established family practice and traditions. A bedwetting five-year-old may be perceived as normal in a family where the parents themselves were not dry before the age of seven. Conversely, in a very organized and obsessively clean family a wet four-year-old may be a disaster.

Our idea of normality is also subject to the vagaries of fashion, as reflected in childcare books. A glance at the huge range of childcare books that have hit the shelves over the past 100 years shows that child-rearing practices vary widely according to the political climate and ideology prevailing at the time they were written. The Victorians apparently thought it right to start potty training as young as three weeks, whereas the permissive sixties produced parents who were happy to leave it to their toddlers to decide when to pee and poo in the right places. In the 1990s we see a whole range of childcare practices and people finally seem to have come round to accepting that there is room for difference, whether it is based on family traditions, cultural variations or the idiosyncratic ideas of parents.

Nevertheless, today's wide range of options does not stop parents looking for a norm, especially when they come up against problems. Nor does it mean that 'anything goes'. Common sense will, of course, tell most parents when something is physically wrong with their child. They worry when a child shows no signs of walking at two or talking at three and they will often seek professional advice. But there are grey areas where all the parents can do is to compare their offspring with their peers or consult a good childcare book.

Issues such as bedwetting, night terrors and school refusal are frequent causes of anxiety and may eventually lead to the involvement of professionals. However if parents reach the stage of enlisting their help, they will rarely be given a simple 'norm' to follow. This is because it is recognized that the solution to a child's problem usually involves wider family-based issues. The extent to which parents regard specific sorts of behaviour in their child as problematic is crucial, as is their real desire to take advice and actually change things. Dreadful though some aspect of family life may seem to an outsider, some people prefer things to stay the same when they realize what changing them could involve.

*Cheryl was seven when she first missed a lot of school. At eight she failed to go for a whole term. Despite major efforts by the school and the local education department, Cheryl simply refused to go to school. Her parents claimed that they had tried everything, but that Cheryl just would not go. She had nothing against school and had plenty of friends.*

*Cheryl and her family were referred for professional help and it emerged that Cheryl's mother had been very depressed for over a year. This seemed to be strongly connected with the couple's marital problems. Cheryl's father was hardly ever at home and Cheryl had become very preoccupied with her mother's welfare. When at school previously she had often been absent-minded and it seemed that she had been wondering about her mother alone at home.*

*Her mother had made two suicide attempts which the parents had not told Cheryl about. Yet Cheryl somehow 'knew' and had decided to become her mother's companion and nurse. She feigned headaches and tummy aches and these provided good reasons for her to stay at home initially. No doctor was consulted. It gradually became a habit and it suited everyone for Cheryl to keep an eye on her mother.*

There are many different reasons for school refusal. In this case it was the child's anxiety about her mother that stopped her going to school. What would have happened to her mother if Cheryl had been 'cured' of school refusal? In some families there is a vested interest in not solving the child's problem, a fear that change might make things worse.

Other families are exactly the opposite. There are parents who insist on getting their children seen by experts for each and every physical and psychological problem. Although very often nobody can find anything wrong with the child this is not greeted with relief by the parents; instead it may be taken as evidence that the doctor is not skilled enough. This leads to further contact with other professionals. Such intense preoccupation with one's children's health and development can have bad effects. Not surprisingly such children often become more anxious and temperamental, which in turn can be seen as 'proof' by the parent that there is really something amiss. This search for concrete evidence that something is wrong might really be a search for what's gone wrong in the parent's or family's past.

## AND SO TO BED . . .

It may be reassuring to realize that childrearing is not a simple question of sticking to rigid norms and that it is important to take into account the dynamics of the family and how it wishes to lead its life. Nevertheless there will always be issues about which it is hard to feel reassured. These issues arouse intense emotions and touch on deep-rooted fears – perhaps because they are often linked to our most basic needs, such as sleep and sex.

### Musical beds

Most childcare books, rightly, deal with sleeping problems at great length. There are even books dedicated entirely to this topic. After all, sleeping problems in younger children are extremely common. The most familiar scenario is the little child who keeps waking at night and the question is always: 'Should I leave her and let her cry?' When the child is older, however, dealing with wakefulness is even trickier, because he can get up on his own and enter his parents' bed.

Whether and when a child should be allowed to sleep regularly in the parental bed is a controversial issue, even though it

is entirely understandable that a child should want to be close to the parents when it is dark. However the longer children sleep in their parents' rooms or beds, the more difficult it is to 'expel them from paradise'.

*Patrick's parents sought professional advice. They wanted to change their entrenched sleeping habits. Patrick, seven years of age, was in the habit of waking up every night just before midnight, around the time his parents would go to bed. He would take his pillow and duvet, move into the parental bedroom and plonk himself down between his parents. He would fall asleep almost immediately and his parents did not have the heart to wake him up. As Patrick was a restless sleeper, Dad would then reluctantly go and camp in his son's bed next door. This bedtime ritual had gone unchallenged for years. Nobody seemed to mind much. And the parents, immensely stressed by having to satisfy the many diverse needs of their two younger children, felt too exhausted to change it.*

Whether one regards this night-time scenario as normal or not depends entirely on one's perspective and level of tolerance. It may well be a necessary transitional stage, for the parents to get some sleep, and the child may sooner or later grow out of it. This does happen. In Patrick's case, however, it did not. Change only occurred when the initial convenience was outweighed by his parents' need to reclaim their privacy – and their growing unease about whether they might be damaging his sexual development. There is no evidence for this, but there is evidence that chronic 'musical beds' can mask underlying family tensions. These normally need to be made explicit before progress can be made or change can occur. Sexual problems between the parents constitute one of the more frequent underlying reasons. The child's presence in the bedroom is tantamount to a contraceptive and, as long as this lasts, the parents can avoid confronting the issue of their difficult sex life.

In other families children may, often without consciously planning to do so, find themselves keeping the peace between their parents. The sensitive child who wakes up in the middle of the night is finely tuned to tensions between the parents and

---

DIY EXERCISE: TRAPPING MONSTERS

---

Monsters, vampires, ghosts and other 'baddies' are often given as reasons for not falling asleep. Here are some ways of 'wiring' the child's bedroom against monsters.

• First design, together with the child, a monster trap.
• Identify potential entry points (windows, doors, fireplaces, etc).
• Think what contraptions or installations need to be constructed to trick the monster.
• Build elaborate monster traps out of nets, trip wires and pulleys.
• Enlist the help of a favourite toy animal. This can be endowed with magic power and placed next to the child at bedtime.
• Examine the evidence the next morning.

Note: Some parents plant pieces of evidence overnight in the trap as proof that the trap is working. If the whole family gets involved in building the construction, the child's fears are shared and fought by everyone.

---

his or her wakeful presence may prevent their arguments from escalating. In this way the child regulates the distance between the parents, perhaps even keeping Mother safe, as Father does not want to have a major confrontation when the child is present. Who, then, needs whom?

Children rarely think of themselves playing this role. As far as they are concerned, they are frightened to sleep on their own: they may have terrible dreams or suffer from night terrors. Parents, not surprisingly, respond by wanting to comfort the child. But this can be done in the child's bedroom, provided that this is what the parents want and if the child's nightly excursions to the parental bed do not serve some other function. There are creative ways of keeping the child in his or her bedroom – if this is the aim. However, doing this and succeeding may mean that the parents no longer have the child as a buffer between themselves in the marital bed . . .

## WHY CHILDREN REGRESS

All parents can expect to deal with a wet bed at some point. When bedwetting is prolonged, help may be sought. However, once again, the bedwetting may be a symptom of a wider family issue, though physical causes need to be excluded. Some children who have previously been dry may, for a time only, revert to bedwetting. In many instances this is a passing phase.

The most common reason for this sort of regression is the arrival of a new baby, about whom a lot of fuss is being made. Suddenly the older child is no longer the centre of the family's universe and needs to learn to share the parents. Not surprisingly, the child attempts to regain everyone's attention – and what could be more logical than acting the baby? Wanting to wear nappies again, soiling and wetting are very concrete representations of the child's wish to be more looked after.

But there are other reasons why children may act younger than their age and the causes may not, in fact, be linked to the arrival of a new sibling. Talking with a baby voice or reverting to temper tantrums can be signs that acting in a babyish way is somehow rewarded by the parents. Some parents, for instance, may wish to delay the growing-up process.

*Tony was nine and not very tall for his age. He had two older brothers, both in their late teens. Tony's nickname at home had always been 'Tiny', partly because of his size and partly because he acted much younger than his age. In school he would play with children at least two or three years younger and the teachers observed that his classmates treated him as if he were a little toy. Soon they started to make fun of him and 'Tiny' felt very unhappy about going to school.*

*He loved it at home, as he was so well looked after. His mother cooked special food for him so that he did not have to chew too much. She put him to bed, always read him a story and stayed with him until he was asleep. He enjoyed nothing better than sitting on his father's lap, often for hours, or being carried around the house by his brothers.*

*When he refused to go to school altogether and professional help was sought, it emerged that his mother had had a series of operations shortly after Tony had been born and was in and out of hospital for the following year. Tony's father was totally overburdened by having to look after three children and still having to go to work. Talking to the therapist, both parents said they felt that Tony had missed out on parental care during his early years and that they had wanted to make up for this. They were not aware that they had 'babied' him.*

Children who get babied often have difficulties outside the home, particularly with their peers. They act the part of 'the little one' because there are usually considerable immediate benefits, such as extra attention from adults. However, rewarding age-inappropriate behaviours can become problematic, as the children grow up much more slowly and, though often very sweet and endearing, get left behind.

In some children signs of regression can point to very serious underlying causes. Some emotionally abused children, whose parents constantly tell them how useless and bad they are, will literally say that they feel 'like a piece of shit'. Not surprisingly, they often start soiling, put their excrement in strategic places or smear it on walls, as 'graffiti' depicting their inner state. Being rubbished from morning to evening, they have no sense of self-worth and often behave outside the home in such a way that other children also turn on them. Similarly, sexually abused children may start soiling and wetting in an (often unconscious) attempt to draw the attention of helpful adults to those parts of the body. Medical examination of a persistently soiling child not infrequently reveals sexual abuse.

## SIBLING RIVALRIES

Most parents hope that their children will grow up liking if not loving one another. It often causes them considerable distress if their offspring squabble and fight repeatedly. But why do some siblings get on, while others don't? Personality clashes or age differences account for some of the problems but if siblings are consistently rivalrous the problem usually goes deeper.

Understandably, a common cause of rivalry or jealousy is the feeling that the parents prefer another child. This may have its roots in the way the birth of this child was handled: the older one may feel neglected or rejected and hate the new arrival, especially if parents virtually apologize for having another baby. Alternatively, they may go to the opposite extreme and try to brainwash the child into believing that having a little companion is the nicest possible thing that could ever have happened.

Rivalry and jealousy may also occur when parents unconsciously favour one child. This may reflect their own experience or birth order. A father who was the first born in his own family and who felt deprived of love after the arrival of a younger brother may in turn identify with his own eldest child and attempt to compensate for the love he never got. Another reason why parents may favour a particular child is because there may be a family likeness to someone special, for example an adored grandmother.

It could, on the other hand, be because the child apparently resembles the parent or because he or she appears to display a particular talent that is linked with some family tradition, such as being artistic or musical. A given child may also be 'special' as the result of a serious illness or because its birth was preceded by a series of miscarriages or even by the death of a child.

> *Harry was the middle child of three brothers. His mother had always been particularly attached to him and this caused considerable rivalry between the brothers. He seemed special to her and she was very protective of him, worrying about the smallest signs of illness. She loved all three children equally and her husband confirmed this. But Harry's brothers simply did not believe this and frequently asked their mother why she loved Harry more than them.*
>
> *Harry was about eight years old when he became aware of this – it didn't feel like a privilege but, rather, a burden. 'Why do you fuss so much, Mum?' he would ask her repeatedly. At that point both parents wondered whether they should tell him that he had been born after three miscarriages and a year to the day after another brother, whose existence had been kept secret,*

*had died – a few hours after he was born. The dead boy had also been named Harry and the living Harry seemed to have become his replacement.*

*The parents sought professional advice and the mother described how even now she would stand at the school gate, waiting for Harry to come out and imagining what it would be like to have the older, dead Harry come out as well. With professional help the secret was brought out into the open and, after a lot of crying all round, the death of the first Harry was acknowledged and finally accepted. This helped the living Harry to be accepted for who he was and decreased the rivalry between himself and his brothers to what the family regarded as a 'normal' level.*

## SELF-FULFILLING PROPHECIES

It has already been suggested that events in the past can cast long shadows. How parents deal with their young children is crucially influenced by their own experiences and by their own wider family. Some parents overdo the common and natural search for familiar traits, be they Dad's, Auntie's or Cousin Joe's. At times parents attribute negative family traits to a child, implying that they might be hereditary and therefore unchangeable.

*When Bill developed facial tics and grimaces at the age of ten his parents' alarm bells went. The mother's brother had developed similar symptoms some eight years before he 'went mad'. Was Bill going to be like him? Thinking back, his parents remembered that he had always been 'different', apart from resembling his uncle physically.*

*When they took Bill to see their doctor they asked, 'Is he going to be a schizophrenic, like his uncle?' Although Bill did not understand exactly what the word meant, he understood that it was something quite worrying. The more concerned his parents became, the more he thought there was something wrong with him. This had the effect, over time, of increasing his doubts about himself, and he became very shy and quiet.*

DIY EXERCISE: WHO DO YOU TAKE AFTER?

Being given an identity as the 'reincarnation' of some mad or bad relative can be horrendous. This exercise may help to relieve you or another family member of this burden.

• Draw your family tree (see page 15).
• Decide who you most resemble.
• Compare your view with those of other family members, e.g. Who does your mother/father/sister etc think you are most like?
• On which of your characteristics is each of these views based?
• Do you agree? Or do you think you are more like someone else?
• Now list all the major features of the person you are meant to be like (such as humour, stubbornness, generosity, dishonesty).
• Once you have compiled a list of at least ten characteristics, tick those which apply to you.
• Compile a list of all the characteristics you possess but which in your opinion the other person does not have.
• Now look at the similarities and differences: do you really take after that person?

Note: As a parent, you can do the same exercise and evaluate whom, if anyone, your child takes after.

This phenomenon is not as uncommon as one might think. There are less dramatic versions, with children having an identity bestowed on them that really belongs to somebody else. If parents insist on it for long enough, there comes a point when the child gives in and exhibits precisely the dreaded trait. Positive expectations can be equally incapacitating. The pressure to follow in the footsteps of a successful parent or grandparent can be a tremendous burden, resulting more often than not in failure to live up to the pre-programmed script.

## Chapter 7

# Coping with teenage excesses

IN THIS CHAPTER WE LOOK AT:
•
WHAT ADOLESCENCE IS ALL ABOUT
•
ADOLESCENT SEXUALITY
•
EATING DISORDERS
•
UNRULY TEENAGERS
•
PROBLEM PARENTS
•
LEAVING HOME

*'Have you tidied up your room, Jack?'*
*'No . . . in a minute.'*
*'Have you tidied up your room yet?'*
*'I said '"in a minute".'*
*'But that was an hour ago.'*
*'Give me a break . . . I said I'd do it.'*
*'You said that yesterday.'*
*'Oh Mum . . . leave me alone.'*
*'No . . . I won't.'*
*'What?'*
*'I said I won't'*
*'Won't what?'*

*'Won't leave you alone.'*
*'This is my room . . . Can't I have any privacy?'*
*'I'll leave you alone if you tidy up your room.'*
*'Yes . . . in a minute.'*
*'Do you want me to get your dad?'*
*'Go ahead.'*
*'Joe, could you please come and tell Jack to tidy up his room?'*
*'Yes . . . in a minute . . .'*

Teenagers can make the family explode like an enormous spot. They can be so sensible one minute and totally unreasonable the next. In response, their parents often switch from being laid back and permissive to utterly rigid and angry a few seconds later. Adolescence is a phase that most families expect to survive rather than enjoy.

## ADOLESCENCE – A TIME OF CHANGE

Adolescence is a time of change: acne, breasts, egos and other things grow. It is also a time of firsts: first cigarette, first sexual experience, first time drunk, first menstruation, first ejaculation . . . Adolescence can be tough for young people and no less difficult for those dealing with them. Adolescents cannot help experimenting with almost anything that comes their way: sex, drugs, gods, pop idols, hairstyles, food. They make mammoth telephone calls, sprinkle their conversation with four-letter words – the list is endless. Everything these youngsters do is excessive: it's all or nothing!

Jane feels that her parents never approve of what she does, while Jack thinks his parents are old-fashioned and boring. The parents themselves cannot do anything to please their offspring. In their daily clashes parents feel provoked by their kids' outrageous behaviour. The kids in turn are outraged by their parents' narrow-mindedness and restrictiveness. The irony is that everyone seems to want peace and quiet, yet no opportunity is missed to turn the sitting room into a battlefield. The parents can never get it right, no matter what they say. Any of the following statements is likely to spark off an argument:

*'I want you to be back by 9pm, Jack.'*
*'I want you to be back by 11pm, Jack.'*
*'I want you to be back by 3am, Jack.'*
*'I want you to be back for breakfast, Jack.'*
*'I don't mind when you're back, Jack, but we want Jane to be home by 1am – she is a girl.'*
*'I don't care when any of you come back.'*
*'Mum thinks you should be back by midnight, but I don't mind if you stay out as long as you like. Still . . . I want you to do what Mum says – otherwise I'll be in trouble.'*

Adolescence seems to be a time of mutual incomprehension between parents and their children. Teenagers have an almost uncanny ability to stir up trouble, not always deliberately, with comments such as:

*'You've always loved Jamie and Jane more than me.'*
*'Come on, Dad, dope is harmless – here, smoke this and see for yourself.'*
*'Dad, you should see what Mum keeps in her handbag!'*
*'Mum, I know you think Ed is a thief and mugger – but I hope you don't mind if he comes and lives with us for a few weeks. His parents have kicked him out and he's got nowhere to go.'*

These and other provocations seem to pour out of the mouths of young people, much to the annoyance of their parents. But it is not simply what they say which leads to trouble: posture, clothing, body odour, hairstyle all communicate moods and states of mind. More than any other age group, adolescents are capable of freezing their parents out with a single look. They specialize in leaving smelly socks in the most unlikely places, and possess unrivalled skill at getting stranded after the last tube or bus has gone.

Parents usually see this type of behaviour as their teenagers wanting to have their cake and eat it, wanting to appear independent whilst remaining dependent. But this is rather one-sided and, as teenagers are quick to point out, it all looks quite different from the young person's perspective. They see a couple of decrepit, middle-aged people, who happen to be their parents and who are inevitably much worse than their friends' parents (their friends incidentally feel it is the other way round). These parents have nothing better to do than make stupid rules and nag. They have no sense of fun when it comes to almost anything the young person reckons is 'wicked' or 'cool'.

In short, there seems to be an ever-widening gap between adolescents and their parents. The gap could be called a 'four-year gap'. This is the phenomenon of parents perceiving their teenagers as being at least two years younger than their actual age, whereas they think of themselves as being at least two years older than their birth certificates indicate. It is hard to bridge this four-year gap, a task which is further complicated by the teenager's rapid alternation between mature and childish behaviour. Adolescence is above all a time of change, and the whole family needs to change if this phase is to be successfully negotiated.

Many arguments with adolescents are extremely predictable, and parents often ask themselves afterwards why they rose to the bait. Teenagers love to argue – they regard it as character-forming. And parents oblige as if it were really serious – a question of life or death. But teenagers blow hot and cold and what is important one minute is entirely 'boring' the next. So, why get excited? Arguments tend to raise the blood pressure and maybe parents get addicted to them too. Perhaps being able to have a good argument reassures the parents that they are still young. Teenagers possibly need that reassurance as well – to check that the parents aren't completely brain-dead yet . . .

So, what is adolescence all about? Given the enormous variation in adolescent behaviour, it is extremely difficult to decide what's normal and what's not. This difficulty is compounded by the fact that families and their expectations differ a great deal – and this has as much to do with culture and class as with specific family dynamics. Teenage pregnancies, for example, whilst usually thought of as undesirable, may be the norm in some families, whereas elsewhere the idea of a girl having sex before she reaches eighteen is unimaginable. A red flag for one family is a green light for another, and many familiar values and rules get turned upside down.

The change from child to teenager can come as a terrible shock for many families. Not so long ago our adolescent children were ten- and eleven-year-olds, often as good as gold, idealizing their parents and thinking that home was best. But only a year or two later, they seem to reject those same parents and claim that they can't wait to leave home. Although the parents know this is designed to challenge and provoke them, they get deeply hurt and wonder what they have done to deserve it.

They need to bear in mind that adolescent girls and boys are in quite a state, with blood flowing apparently uncontrollably up and down their bodies, resulting in blushing, periods and unwanted erections. All this can be embarrassing and disturbing and it is not surprising that parents often end up on the receiving end of their teenager's distress. Meanwhile, as far as the parents are concerned, they haven't done anything other than be the safe and understanding repositories of their children's trials and tribulations.

## ADOLESCENCE – A TRIAL FOR EVERYONE?

Not all teenagers go through dreadful stormy phases. Some families are spared most of the excesses described above and others get none of them at all, so much so that they worry that their son or daughter is missing out on something. Generally parents needn't be worried about this, though one does occasionally come across young people who feel that they cannot afford to experiment with adolescence.

*Jimmy, the oldest of three children, felt he had to step into his father's shoes after his sudden departure. Jimmy was only eight years old at the time. His mother looked to him for support and he became the unofficial head of the family at a very tender age. His younger brother and sister obeyed him and he also started feeling responsible for his mother. At fourteen he took on weekend jobs to contribute to the family budget. He socialized little with his peers; instead he helped his siblings with their homework and studied hard himself. He aimed to go to university so that he could eventually get a high-powered job which would enable him to continue to support his family.*

*When Jimmy suddenly developed severe back pain at the age of fifteen his mother became very concerned. The doctors could find nothing physically wrong and Jimmy himself felt guilty about not being able to help at home. However he was flat out for weeks and his mother and siblings looked after him.*

*Lying on his back Jimmy viewed family life from an entirely different perspective. He was surprised to find that his mother was much more competent than he had imagined – and so were his younger siblings. Jimmy relaxed and extended his bed rest. He caught up with a lot of school work and was able to talk to his mother about how hard it had been for him to be the backbone of the family for all those years and how much he felt everyone had been leaning on him for support. At some point he told his mother that he had not been surprised when his back eventually gave in – with all the pressures on him. Over the following weeks the family discussed how the pressures could be more evenly distributed. Jimmy recovered fully and the family found a new balance which enabled Jimmy to enjoy life as a teenager . . .*

Teenagers often have very mixed feelings. Whilst behaving as if they were totally irresponsible, they may show many indirect signs of being very concerned about the welfare of their parents.

Illness is one way in which these chronic helpers can make their own needs known. When children miss out on teenage activities and relationships their development is halted – even if they seem very mature. Some of these children postpone their adolescence until it is safer to experiment. This can be as much as twenty years later when some fairly outrageous behaviour may lead people to say that they're going through a 'second adolescence'.

Try the exercise opposite. The goals may seem banal, but it requires small steps and some moderate successes to persuade teenagers and their parents that change can take place – however hopeless the situation may seem.

DIY EXERCISE: TAKE ANOTHER LOOK AT YOUR TEENAGER

If you are at your wits' end with your teenage son or daughter ask a good family friend to help you with this exercise.
- First ask your friend to write down all the positive points about your teenage son or daughter.
- Get your friend to identify the characteristics your teenager has in common with each parent.
- Now study the list. You may not agree with each individual point. You may also think that your son or daughter always puts on a performance when your friend is around. Never mind. The fact that your friend has found positive points – for example that he or she can be interesting to talk to, thoughtful, or polite – means that your son or daughter can't be all bad!
- Concentrate and build on the positive points and use them to define a small, achievable goal. Do not pick negative or unrealistic goals. The aim is to make things more positive! Examples of achievable small goals are:
  - spending 20 minutes once a week sitting in the same room and discussing a neutral subject
  - watching a favourite TV programme together
  - going for a short outing to a place of mutual interest
  - saying 'thank you' to each other twice a week
  - listening to his/her music once a fortnight.

TEENAGE SEXUALITY AND HOW NOT TO HANDLE IT

It may be an alarming thought for many families, but teenagers have the power to turn their parents into grandparents. Not that having sex is on your average teenager's mind all the time. In fact many young teenagers are not particularly interested in having sex, but practically all of them have sexual feelings or fantasies. Acting on these feelings is quite another matter and much depends on how the family handles them.

Parents often assume that sex education has already taken

place at school – some years ago. This absolves them from responsibility for a task many parents feel uncomfortable with, but they rarely bother to find out what their teenagers actually know. Should the parents talk openly with their son or daughter about intercourse, masturbation and homosexuality? Should the parents initiate such conversations – or should they wait for the teenager to ask? Should the parents ask to be informed about their teenager's sexual activities? Should they turn a blind eye or make a point of finding out?

Sadly, or happily, there is no universal way of getting it 'right' but parents can try to avoid some of the major mistakes. Here then are some of the DON'TS:

DON'T assume that your son or daughter knows the facts of life even though this may be on the school curriculum.

DON'T fail to give them opportunities to find out about safe sex, contraception, VD and AIDS.

DON'T give them the message that sex cannot be talked about.

DON'T make them feel it's wrong to have sexual feelings.

DON'T spy on them.

DON'T pry into their private letters or secret diaries.

DON'T say you don't care when, where or with whom they have sex.

There are many other DON'TS which may be important to one family but irrelevant to the one next door. Each reader may have his or her own taboo area: sex is still the most difficult topic to discuss in public.

Teenagers may test out some of their sexual feelings by practising on their parents. Whilst they usually find it impossible to believe that their parents still have sex, this does not stop them relating to their mother or father at times as if they were sexual beings. A daughter may flirt with her father to explore her impact on the other sex with a safe man. Her father may deliberately avoid hugging her in order not to inadvertently touch her breasts. Some teenagers walk around the house half-naked and call their parents prudes when they tell them to dress properly. Teenagers can be provocative and at times they are not even aware of it: much of their behaviour is not deliberate – and that applies equally to their sexuality.

Allowing one's teenage children's sexuality to develop without either ignoring it, or interfering with it, is very difficult. But this is an aspect of family life which can cause serious problems later on if it is not handled fairly and sympathetically.

*Jake was the youngest of three children. He lived with his divorced mother, two older sisters and grandmother. The one thing all these women had in common was that they hated men. This did not make things particularly easy for Jake when he hit puberty. Up to then he had been spared the condemnations reserved for men because he was 'only' a boy. The only other male in the house was the family cat which had not only been neutered but had also been given a female name: Jackie.*

*As Jake's mother and sisters waltzed naked through the house, discussing their periods and bosoms, he felt more and more ashamed. It really got bad when his sisters burst into the bathroom to make fun of his 'thingie'. This happened a few times and, as there was no lock on the bathroom door, Jake barricaded himself in. Even though his mother and sisters told him how much they loved him, he slowly began to feel that being a man made him worthless. He now understood why his father had left home ten years ago.*

This fairly extreme example shows how unfinished business from the past can get recycled in the present, with the danger of a growing man turning into a woman-hater just like his father.

Children's sexual development is a delicate subject and there is no perfect way of handling it. Much depends on the relationship between parents and the young person. Sex may be a taboo subject in certain families, for a variety of reasons. Social inhibitions, old-fashioned values, dark and murky secrets to do with incest in the past, a poor view of women, experiences of violent men – the list of possible explanations is endless.

If sex remains a taboo subject in a family, what message is conveyed to young people? Will they think that sex should not or cannot be talked about? These young people will then start speculating as to why sex is a taboo area: because it's dirty, because it's secret, because it's associated with bad memories? Not discussing sex openly leads to fantasies and secretive behaviour. On the whole, clear, open communication tends to be much more helpful than hints and innuendo.

But how do you tackle something that may have been a taboo subject for generations? Here is one of many possible ways. Parents can break the ice by acknowledging the obvious: 'In our family sex seems to be a taboo subject . . . I'm not happy about this and I would like to change it . . .' Naming one's own inhibitions or hesitations is the first step towards openness and honesty.

Many parents have some sexual feelings about their teenage children. And the same is true of teenagers about their parents. Having such feelings or fantasies is very different from acting on them: a sexual relationship between a parent and a child – of whatever age – is one of the most damaging experiences a young person can have. It leaves her or him utterly confused, abused in the name of love, betrayed by the person or people they most trusted.

Such sexual abuse is usually kept secret from the rest of the family, a pact frequently sealed by physical threats or emotional blackmail. Unfortunately there are still some parents, mostly fathers, who believe it was good for their teenage daughters to have sex with them. In lame self-defence such a father might claim that he was seduced by his thirteen-year-old daughter, adding to her distress by making her feel responsible for what happened. However much we, as outsiders, know that the sole responsibility for the abuse lies with the perpetrator, the victim, torn apart by years of mis-taken love, often cannot help feeling guilty.

Having a parent in whom she can confide, who believes her and who can protect her, will help her deal with one of the worst traumas anyone can suffer. Unfortunately many abused teenagers find it very difficult to establish trust with anyone, having been so bitterly disappointed by those who were meant to love them unconditionally.

## TO EAT OR NOT TO EAT . . .

Adolescents just cannot get it right in the eyes of their parents: inevitably they eat too little, too much, or too much of the wrong thing. And, of course, as far as the adolescents themselves are concerned, their parents cannot get it right either: they fuss too much or too little. The more the parents fuss over food the more problematic the eating becomes. Or is it the other way round? The more abnormally the adolescent eats, the fussier the parents become.

Eating disorders can occur at any age, but serious ones most commonly start during adolescence. With the redistribution of fat to different parts of the anatomy, the ever-changing body can become a source of confusion for the teenager. Fashions and peer pressure, together with emerging sexual feelings, all combine to weaken an already shaky self-image. To cope with these stresses some teenagers either stuff or starve themselves.

*Steve's friends could not believe how much he ate. He was constantly hungry and he seemed to be putting on a pound per day. He was only thirteen and he already weighed 13 stone. His parents consulted a paediatrician who suggested a diet, but Steve simply would not stick to it: what he loved most was chips, chocolate and ice-cream. The paediatrician then suggested that Steve compile an eating diary recording when he ate what, and in what sort of quantities.*

*A fortnight later the family had the necessary information: Steve ate most between 6 and 8pm and on weekends. Steve and the family were asked how they could join forces and find something to replace food during these times. Initially the family drew a total blank – they had not done anything together for years. Worried about his weight and the long-term risk to his health, however, they were prepared to change their life patterns and instituted an elaborate rota system whereby each parent would find some physical activity to keep him busy during these times. Mother went swimming with Steve three times a week, Father and Steve joined a badminton club and played on two other late afternoons and on Sunday mornings.*

*Steve became fit very quickly and lost a considerable amount of weight – as did his parents who had both been overweight. Steve and his parents got to know each other much better and, as he began to feel more at ease in his body, he became more interested in sport at school. Six months later he represented his school at badminton and swimming and had a string of friends all queuing up to do sports with him at weekends. His parents, having themselves developed a new taste for physical activity, now remained fit by going swimming and playing badminton.*

It is not always easy to replace comfort eating with another activity, although there are many similar success stories. When teenagers do not like the idea of being seen as sexual beings they may try to make themselves as unattractive as possible – and this can be done by over-eating or self-starvation.

Amongst a number of other issues, growing up means having to come to terms with one's sexuality. Some teenagers react like Peter Pan – by refusing to grow up. This may be connected with the way sexuality has been handled in the family and what role models have been available. For example, if a daughter has witnessed her mother being humiliated through years of marriage, she may not wish ever to get into the same position. This could lead her to try to be different from her mother – perhaps by being asexual. This could take the form of behaving as a tomboy, or neglecting her appearance, dressing shabbily, disregarding personal hygiene and cultivating a 'man-repellent' body odour. Another way of refusing to grow up is to stunt one's sexual development by self-starvation.

When it comes to eating disorders there are also other forces at work. In Chapter 2 we saw how Stephanie's hunger strike could be seen as a way of stating her wish to be independent – at some considerable cost. Self-starvation in adolescence is not uncommon and there are many reasons for it, some to do with the family and some not. Here we shall only concentrate on the 'family factor'.

Anorexic teenagers, most of them girls – less than ten per cent of them are boys – usually come from loving families. In fact some of these families are too loving and this becomes too much for the thirteen- or fourteen-year-old who can no longer tolerate her parents' preoccupation with her at a time when she herself is overwhelmed by the arrival of puberty. As she finds it very difficult in her 'loving' family to tell her parents to leave her alone, she does it indirectly and usually not deliberately – but much more concretely.

When living in an environment without any boundaries, where one feels utterly controlled by 'love' and the expectation of having to reciprocate in kind, one's body is perhaps the only thing one can be in control of. Not eating sometimes seems the only possible way of saying 'no' to one's parents, not unlike the six-month-old who, refusing to eat solids, tells his parents without words that he can say 'no'. This painful lesson may need to be repeated in adolescence when issues of independence and autonomy are dramatically revived.

Anorexia nervosa may in the later stages require medical intervention, such as the infusion of intravenous fluids and electrolytes, to save the young person's life. Only when the physical state of the anorexic has been stabilized can psychological therapies be successfully implemented. Family therapy has proved a very effective method of helping the family and the anorexic find ways of confronting typical adolescent issues without resorting to going on hunger strike or having to force-feed the emaciated teenager. This means in practice that family life is going to be less 'nice' but also much less dangerous: loud arguments will replace quiet self-destruction.

## WHY SOME TEENAGERS SEEK BAD COMPANY

Growing up inevitably involves increased socializing with one's peers. Making contact with the outside world carries the risk of coming under what parents call 'bad influences'. These so-called bad influences can be used by parents as convenient excuses for their own children's appalling behaviour. 'It's not our fault ... it's the company he keeps nowadays...' is a frequent refrain. The question is: why do some teenagers seek out bad company when others don't? Is it just bad luck?

*Nobody was surprised when Connor was thrown out of his expensive private school. There had been plenty of warnings and it really seemed that he had been pushing his luck. The youngest of three children and the only boy, he had been both the pride and the disappointment of his parents. Distinctly middle class, with respectable professions, they had been somewhat amused when Connor had first adopted a strong working-class accent. In line with this, he tended to mix with rough kids from the area and had few friends in his private school, regarding them as sissies. His local friends came to the family home every night, played deafening music and told vulgar jokes. His parents were quite horrified.*

*When Connor got caught up in fights with other kids and the police stopped him for carrying a knife, his parents were in despair. It was only when they sought professional advice from a family therapy clinic that they started making some of the connections. Connor's dad talked about his own adolescence, remembering that he had developed a passion for boxing. He recounted times when he had used his boxing skills to defend himself against a local gang.*

*Connor had never heard about this and when he asked how his father's father had handled this, there was a long silence. In fact Connor suddenly realized that he knew nothing about his grandfather and that his father had always been very reluctant*

SINCE TIMOTHY'S BEEN SEEING HIS NEW FRIEND'S, HE'S TURNED INTO A REAL ANGEL

DIY EXERCISE: CONNECTING WITH YOUR TEENS

Your adolescence may seem very distant. If you want to understand what your teenage children are going through, try to connect with it by answering the questions below.

- Remember when you were a teenager (aged thirteen to eighteen):
  - What was the worst thing you ever did?
  - Did your parents find out about it?
  - What was their response?
  - Who was crosser, your mum or your dad?
  - Were they right to be upset or did they over-react?
  - Did you want to upset them?
  - What was the most annoying thing that your mother/father could say to you?
  - How does that connect with what your son/daughter finds most annoying about you as a parent?
  - Which of your teenage son's/daughter's friends and interests do you share now, as an adult?
  - Which would you like if you were a teenager now?
- Evaluate your answers:
  - Is your teenager any less distant now?
  - Can you understand him or her any better?
- Start talking to your teenager about what you have in common (rather than continuing to dwell on your differences).

*to talk about him. Now Connor finally learned that his father came from very humble circumstances, the only child of a single mother, with a father who occasionally entered his life, drunk and jobless, and then disappeared for years on end.*

*Connor's father had never forgiven his own father and, embarking on a career as a lawyer, had vowed to give his children a very different upbringing. In his efforts to erase his past he had desperately tried to forget everything, including his working-class accent. Connor's behaviour had brought it all back.*

Teenagers are often much more sensitive than their parents give them credit for. At times it almost seems that they have extra-sensory perception, the way they pick up on issues that have never been openly talked about. However all this is slightly less mysterious than it seems. Having lived with their parents for all or most of their lives, teenagers learn to read between the lines. They observe the way their parents avoid certain topics or discussions about their own childhood. This intrigues the teenagers and often leads them to experiment with some of the taboos, if only to find out why the parents are so cagey.

This creates a problem that parents of teenagers are only too familiar with: the more they do not want their offspring to inquire into certain matters, the more likely they are to do precisely that.

Looked at from a different angle, it is often as if the parents unconsciously want the young person to re-enact something they themselves were never allowed to do. Connor's parents' behaviour indirectly encouraged him to reconnect with a forgotten part of his father's previous life. Making connections between the past and the present is often the first step to resolving a current family issue.

The unruly adolescent is quite common. Some 'bad boys' are there to replace bad men or even to reincarnate them. Others cannot help but live up to the family expectation that boys are bad or have to go through a bad patch. Until a family realizes that this is a 'script' rather than a truth, the pattern will keep repeating itself.

## PUNISHMENTS AND SANCTIONS

What can parents do when teenagers break the rules? Many of the strategies used with younger children no longer work – teenagers can see straight through hollow threats of punishment or unashamed bribery. Physical punishment cannot work in the long run because violence breeds violence, and because many adolescents are stronger than their parents. If hit, they can hit back and nasty fights will ensue, with a third party, most likely mother or a sibling, caught in the crossfire.

'Paradoxing' one's adolescent children is another strategy that parents sometimes try. This involves telling the teenager to do precisely the opposite of what the parent really wants in the hope that the teenager's compulsion to oppose anything his parents say will lead to the secretly desired result. For example, a mother involved in an endless series of shouting matches with her permanently disobedient daughter may repeatedly tell her to scream louder and be more verbally abusive. As the daughter cannot obey anything her mother tells her, she will need to be quiet and non-abusive if she wants to disobey her . . .

Clever though such manoeuvres may seem, the kids soon cotton on and paradox back – taking the parents' instructions literally, doing what they told them to do, and then blaming them for the result by saying 'Well, you told me to do it . . .'

Paradox and punishment don't work terribly well in the long run. A more successful way of teaching your son or daughter the consequences of breaking rules is to impose sanctions which limit the availability of something the young person is fond of. Such withdrawal of privileges may include not being allowed to watch a favourite TV programme, being grounded for a short time, missing a sports event or getting no pocket money. Sanctions are usually a diplomatic means of settling a conflict and they can be negotiated. If the young person knows what is in store if he breaks a particular rule he thereby takes full responsibility for the outcome. Teenagers can be very good at making out that they don't mind a specific sanction in order to tempt a parent to lift it. But there is little point in adults imposing sanctions if they lift them a minute later.

## PROBLEM PARENTS

There is much talk about problem adolescents and little about problem parents; yet they are probably just as common. Some parents find their offspring's adolescence a trial because of what it stirs up in them, and it can become apparent that *they* are the problem rather than the children.

**Jealous parents**

Jealous parents present considerable problems for their teen-age children. Many parents will deny that they could ever feel envious but in the same breath mention that they had a hard upbringing and that it wouldn't do their sons or daughters any harm if they did not have quite so much fun.

A father, for example, may make continuous references to his adolescence, how he had to earn money and do the house-work in the evenings and weekends. Such talk usually falls on deaf ears and when the teenage children eventually pluck up courage to accuse their father of 'just being envious that we have a better life than you', all hell can break loose.

If the mother believes that her children deserve to have a good time she will find it very difficult to take a position in the ensuing conflict: if she backs the children she will enrage her husband further; if she backs him the children will despise her for siding with their father just to keep the peace. In the heat of the moment there is little one can do. But it is possible to discuss the issues when the situation is calmer.

The most difficult step is for the envious parent to acknowl-edge their own envy. Once that is done, the battle is half won. The parent then needs to consider the question: 'Why should children not have a better childhood than their parents had?' And this leads to the further question: 'How can I start to take pleasure in my children's pleasure?'

**Competitive parents**

Some parents compete with their children. A mother may, deliberately or even without realizing it, get involved in a contest with her daughter. She may wear an identical hairstyle, use the same make-up, wear similar clothes and then be ex-tremely pleased to be mistaken by some male for her daugh-ter's sister. Likewise, some fathers cannot bear their teenage sons to be better at tennis, chess or bird-watching and they compete with them, risking a heart attack or public humilia-tion in the process.

Rivalry between the generations can reach frightening pro-portions, with ageing parents behaving like teenagers. Being overtaken by your offspring produces pride in most parents

WHY CAN'T YOU
BE LIKE ALL THE OTHERS
AND HAVE ONE THROUGH
YOUR EAR?

and despair in others. The latter reaction often has a lot to do with unfulfilled ambitions and missed opportunities. When these feelings are not acknowledged by parents they prevent them enjoying the young person's successes and may eventually become a burden. Some adolescents feel they must not outshine their elders and consequently stunt their own development with the effect that their parents feel slightly less bad about their own shortcomings. Self-sacrifice in teenagers is rare but it does happen.

**Dependent parents**
There are some parents, often lonely and physically unwell, who make increased demands on their children at a time when their growing independence threatens to make them less available to help at home. Having been groomed all their lives to become their parents' companions, these youngsters cannot help feeling sorry for them. The result is that, out of loyalty, they forfeit their adolescence.

These 'young grown-ups' are almost inevitably described as 'very good and very kind' and are bound to be the envy of those parents who are involved in daily domestic warfare with their 'impossible' teenagers. However behaving like honorary spouses makes teenagers age prematurely. This results in them getting teased by their peers whom they, in turn, find boring (as they are only used to adult company) and this further increases their isolation from their contemporaries.

*Patrick, in his late teens, would only go out with his parents. The three of them were well known in the neighbourhood. Three times a day they would set out for their walks and shopping excursions. Arm in arm, they left home, always at the same time, with Patrick carrying anything that needed to be carried – the very model of a close family.*

*Patrick had no friends and he did not seem to mind. He had left school at sixteen after years of being bullied and had not pursued his education any further. He spent a lot of time in his room, curtains drawn, listening to music and reading books. His parents were worried about his isolation and hoped he would get married one day. Everyone was shocked when, one evening, Patrick smashed up his room. This was followed by Patrick's first encounter with psychiatrists who diagnosed him as 'psychotic'. His parents prepared themselves to care for him long-term, at home . . .*

Adolescents may have to pay a heavy price for being their parents' companion. At worst they may be turned into a chronic 'nurse' or 'patient'. Nursing a parent can be a lifetime's occupation and, when the parent eventually dies, there may be regrets and an empty space that seems unfillable. When it happens the other way round, as in the case of Patrick, the parent or parents are turned into nurses and their son or daughter can become their 'patient' and lifetime project. Neither outcome is desirable for any family, but may be tolerated because the idea of the child leaving home is too unbearable.

Adolescence marks the transition between childhood and adulthood, between dependence and independence, so it is only natural for both parents and teenagers to have mixed feelings when it comes to leaving the nest. Parents know that, once the last child has gone, they may initially feel a sense of relief, but their departure will force them to reorganize and reassess their lives. They will have to contemplate being a

DIY EXERCISE: PARENTAL DISAPPEARING ACTS

Have you ever thought of just walking out on your impossible teenagers? Of course you have, but then you thought of all the damage they could cause in your absence, both to themselves and your property and you then probably dismissed the idea as too risky. But you don't have to walk out in the heat of the moment: you can do a Parental Disappearing Act. This is a planned strategy to give your teenage children the message that you have a life of your own and that this is none of their business. Once a week both parents do the following:

• Decide on a 'secret outing' on a specific day.
• Leave a note on the kitchen table saying: 'We have gone out, will be back late.'
• Leave the house without the children noticing.
• Go to a place where the children are unlikely to locate you and spend the evening.
• Make sure nobody else, especially other family members, knows where you've gone.
• On your return, do not let your children know where you've been.
• Answer all questions by simply saying:
  'That's between your mother and me' and/or
  'That's between your father and me.'
• Repeat these outings once a week, but on different evenings, so that they are unpredictable.

This exercise can have dramatic results. The children won't like it because they will feel excluded. At the same time they may feel reassured that their parents have a life of their own, going to mysterious places. The outings, surrounded by secrecy, may increase the parents' awareness of what it is like to be a couple and may give them a taste of the freedom (or boredom) they will enjoy once their children have left the nest.

couple again. If they have only stayed together 'for the sake of the children', as so many claim, then the time is ripe for a major family crisis.

When is the right time to leave home? This depends on many different factors: finance, culture, health, family traditions, housing . . . and so on. There are no strict guidelines except that each family needs to be aware that this is a major issue which should be discussed regularly and openly. Leaving home suddenly, walking out without warning or in a temper, usually leaves unfinished business behind. Impulsive home-leavers often return, if not weeks then years later. They move back in with the family, sometimes at a fairly advanced age, in the hope that next time round they can leave more 'organically' after proper discussion and negotiation.

## ADOLESCENCE – A TIME OF EXTREMES

Is it right for parents to play games with their growing children? Probably not, but at times – *in extremis* – they may need to resort to unusual strategies. It is important to give teenage children the message that their parents can look after themselves and are even – still! – capable of having some exciting times. Whichever way one communicates this, it must surely come as a relief to young people preparing to leave home to see that their ageing parents can look after each other and do not require constant 'supervision'. It allows young people to concentrate on their own lives.

Adolescence is a major transition and if it is negotiated more or less successfully then young and old can move together into the next phase. What, then, constitutes a successful outcome? Broadly speaking, when both parents and children manage to find an acceptable balance between being prepared for independence whilst wishing to keep some links. What this looks like in practice will very much depend on what different families regard as an acceptable norm.

It is probably a contradiction in terms to talk about a 'normal' adolescence as there are so many ups and downs. We know that teenagers can be delinquent and come into conflict with the law and that this may be an indication that they have not learned some of the home rules or that, if they tested them, no sanctions followed. We also know that the majority of teenage troublemakers turn into very decent and law-abiding citizens. So there is hope. At the other end of the spectrum we know that most shy and reserved adolescents are likely to grow out of these phases. And we also know that life after adolescence is not necessarily the calm after the storm . . .

## Chapter 8

# Mid-life escapades and divorce melodramas

IN THIS CHAPTER WE LOOK AT:

•

## THE EMPTY NEST AND ITS CONSEQUENCES

•

## MID-LIFE CRISES

•

## SECRET AND OPEN AFFAIRS

•

## SEPARATION AND DIVORCE

•

## STEP-FAMILIES

The fairytale about two people falling in love at first sight, getting married and living happily ever after is not based on any present-day reality. Many couples no longer have to wait seven years for the famous itch to occur: about one-third of marriages end in divorce; many more involve temporary separations; while others deteriorate without actually ending. In theory, changes in legislation and social attitudes have made it both easier and more acceptable to quit when the time seems right. Not many people have to endure a lifetime of subjugation or misery. In practice, however, many relationships continue when it would seem in everyone's interest that they should stop. Such relationships cause all parties concerned, and particularly children, much distress.

This chapter explores why people stay together, how relationships can get stale and what can be done about it. It examines how to make things easier when the parental relationship breaks down and how families cope with divorce and remarriage.

## THE EMPTY NEST AND ITS CONSEQUENCES

Once the children have been launched, a new phase starts for the family. The parents, now somewhere between their mid-forties and mid-sixties, have to tackle a number of tasks:

– getting 'remarried'
– finding new ways of relating to their grown-up children
– accepting their children's choice of partner
– preparing for grandparenthood
– managing their own ageing parents.

**Rethinking roles**
Some families find it easier than others to adjust to their children leaving home. Often the parents will have looked forward to this moment. They will have made plans to do all those things which were hard to do when the children were still at home. With their new-found freedom such couples will be able to occupy every minute of the day and renew their own relationship as a twosome.

In other families, where the parents have lived through the children, the situation will be quite different. The departure of the children will leave a sudden void because those who have concentrated more or less exclusively on their parenting role often do so at the expense of developing their own marital relationship. Faced with an empty nest, their own lives seem empty and they take a second look at each other and wonder, now that the children are gone, whether they have anything else left in common.

Such 'retired' parents are in for a difficult time: they are faced with either having to 'get married again' or else contemplating separation. These difficult decisions can be delayed, sometimes indefinitely, by the intervention of their grown-up children who may bring them out of this 'retirement' by providing them with more parenting tasks: they can produce a grandchild and involve the grandparents actively in the baby's care. Or the grown-up child can come back home, having dropped out of college or being heartbroken after a stormy love affair that has gone wrong.

*Joshua, the youngest of three and the last to leave home, went to university at the age of eighteen. During the first year he would come home every weekend, allegedly because he did not like his accommodation. His parents were happy to have him home – it was as if he had never left. His mother would cook all the things he had liked as a child and his father would go every Saturday with Joshua to watch their favourite football team play. On Sunday night his parents would drive him 200 miles to his university and he would arrive there with 'provisions' to last him for the rest of the week.*

*During his second year at university Joshua met a girl and had his first sexual experience. Now his accommodation no longer bothered him and he only went home once that term. He received frequent telephone calls from his mother, asking whether he was eating properly and letting him know that 'We are missing you very much'. When he came home for Christmas, his parents warned him about getting too involved with his girlfriend. He did not listen. He went back to university in early January and the parents heard nothing from him for weeks.*

*After a month the parents decided to visit him and to meet his girlfriend. The reception was frosty and both parents regarded her as very unsuitable. They did not stop talking about their son for the whole of the next week, wondering where they had gone wrong. They tried to telephone him repeatedly, but he did not reply to their messages. He did not come home for the Easter break. Joshua's mother became very depressed and his father sent a telegram requesting him to come back urgently 'to cheer up your mother'.*

*When Joshua saw his mother he was very upset and felt guilty. He started his weekly home visits again. Six weeks later he told his parents that his girlfriend had left him – she thought he was a 'Mummy's boy'. As his mother recovered, it was now Joshua's turn to feel depressed. He felt unable to return to university and asked for a year off.*

When grown-up children return to live with their parents, often years after they have left home, they rarely do this in a conscious effort to rescue their parents' relationship. From their point of view something has gone wrong in their lives and there seems to be nowhere else to go. When they knock at their parents' door they may or may not be welcomed with open arms, depending on whether the parents have managed to rearrange their lives in order to move on.

If this has not happened then the return of the 'lost' son or daughter may not be unwelcome – despite words to the opposite effect. Most parents say they want their children to lead independent lives. However, perhaps without realizing it, they are quite capable of giving a double message and encouraging renewed dependence. When the needs of one or both parents 'fit' those of the young person no obstacles are put in the way of a 'happy reunion'. However, whilst this may be a reasonable short-term solution, it does set back the development not only of the young person, but also of the parents who are now back in their old roles . . .

So, what should be done? Parents can be faced with a considerable dilemma in this situation. On the one hand they see their grown-up child asking for a roof over his or her head – and possibly requesting more parenting. If they give in, they risk setting back by years the young person's growth towards independence. On the other hand, if they turn him or her away, they may then have nightmares about the young person sleeping rough or ending up in an institution. Parents faced with such a dilemma have to weigh up not only what's best for their offspring but also what's best for them. Their own relationship may be going through a difficult patch and the return of the son or daughter might help to stabilize it. On the other hand it might upset it. Moreover, having got used to the novel experience of peace and quiet after many stormy years, the last thing they want is to have this disturbed by new – and old – demands being made on them.

It is usually difficult to evaluate how desperate the young person is for a roof over his or her head. And does it need to be the parental roof? Some children who left home early and abruptly may need to come back home over and over again – to effect a more natural separation.

This was hardly the case with Joshua, in the example just given, who may have become too addicted to his home comforts, with the result that he returned there at the slightest sign of distress. How will this help him to cope on his own? In such a situation parents have to assess whether more long-term progress can be made by discouraging any attempts to re-enter the old familiar life. However when parents find it difficult to live without their children they will receive their 'lost' son (or daughter) with open arms and this message will be quickly picked up by the young person.

Nervous breakdowns, in their various forms, are frequent reasons for returning to the parental home. Seeing their adult child in major distress will give the parents little option but to take him or her in – at least for a short time. But then plans need to be made about what should happen next, to avoid contributing to the young person's state becoming 'chronic'. Many nervous problems in young adults are 'home-grown' and therefore not always best tackled by remaining at home, as this can encourage regression and infantilization. However, throwing a disturbed young person out of the home, with nowhere to go, is rarely therapeutic and usually destructive.

At times it seems that the only choice is between home and hospital – and neither option appears right. This is where relatives or friends can help, by providing a halfway house. Independent from the parents and yet connected with the family, away from home and yet sheltered, the young person has a chance to find their own feet in their own time. For those without willing family or friends there are halfway homes, some of which are funded by local authorities. They provide the shelter for young people who cannot cope at home and cannot cope by themselves in the outside world, helping them and their families to negotiate the transition from home to outside world which often takes years.

## Adding spice to mid-life

Those semi-retired parents who have no son or daughter to rescue them from boredom may want to take a second look at their partner. Has the relationship become too predictable? Is there any hope of injecting some excitement? Surprising one another, deviating from familiar lines, may be exactly what the relationship needs at this point.

I THOUGHT A BIT OF RUBBER MIGHT SPICE THINGS UP IN BED - SO I BOUGHT A NEW HOT WATER BOTTLE

Being prepared to try again presupposes that there is goodwill and not too much disappointment. Couples who have waited for years to separate once the children have left home may be unwilling to give it another go. Yet there are a surprising number of couples who, despite having said they will, do not separate once their children have gone. There may be good reasons for this, such as illness, housing or lack of finance. At other times it may be reawakened friendship and affection. But often it is another major factor that keeps people together – the fear of loneliness.

### DIY EXERCISE: REHEARSING SPONTANEITY

Surprising someone who knows you inside out may be a tall order after all these years. It requires spontaneity, but learning how to be spontaneous sounds like a contradiction in terms. Having said that, there are a few practical steps you can take. But be careful and take the steps one at a time.

**Stage 1: Safe spontaneity**
- Think of some old habits, such as where you sit, what you always watch on TV, or which side of the bed you sleep on.
- Try breaking these habits: don't sit on 'your' chair, or sleep on 'your' side of the bed or watch 'your' TV programme.
- Tell your partner that you are doing this because you want change, and encourage him or her to change too.

**Stage 2: Playful spontaneity**
- Make a pact with your partner: for a fortnight you should each do one spontaneous thing each day, something slightly unusual – but without telling the other what it is.
- At the end of each day you and your partner have to guess what the spontaneous thing was that the other did!

**Stage 3: Serious spontaneity**
Once you have successfully negotiated the first two stages, you can now graduate and become seriously spontaneous – though this does not exclude the use of humour!
- Practise being moderately outrageous (without putting yourself or anyone else at risk).
- Think of yourself as the worst ham actor/actress the world has ever seen. Over-act in the safety of your home! If your own imagination lets you down:
  - try a really silly walk
  - put a mask on or a silly hat
  - make your right hand have a silly conversation with your left hand
  - talk with a foreign accent, maybe like a German officer, an Italian ski-instructor or a French filmstar.
    - Make your partner laugh. If s/he cries you've got it wrong!

WHY PEOPLE STAY TOGETHER: TWO IS COMPANY

Having been together for many years can be habit-forming and
the prospect of not having someone to moan at may be worse
than continuing the kitchen sink battles until one of the partners dies. Staying together as a solution to loneliness works for
some – and not for others. It depends on one's past experiences, one's current options and future hopes. This is how
Sally put it:

> *My mother divorced my father when I was fifteen . . . I was an
> only child . . . I felt lonely, even more so when my father had
> left. My mother never mixed with people. I was all she had. I felt
> guilty when I left home at eighteen to get a job. When I came to
> London I felt lonely. I didn't want to end up like my mother.*
>
> *Then I met Pete. He had a nice flat and he did not mind me
> moving in. We had three children and that kept me busy. It was
> only when they left that I noticed how much I had relied on
> them. Now I suddenly realized that we had been leading
> separate lives. I have often thought of leaving him and
> becoming independent. But then I think of my mother, all alone.
> And what I would miss most is not being in bed next to another
> person – knowing there is someone there.*

How many marriages or relationships are based on habit and
needing to know that someone else is there? Probably a great
many – and that may be good enough for a lot of couples in the
later phases of their lives. They are caught up in lonely partnerships, with separate lives and very little interaction. But the idea
of being all alone seems more frightening than remaining in a
semi-detached relationship with at least the possibility of some
human contact. In order to make things bearable some
couples in their mid-years will change the nest: they may move
or completely alter their home.

Whole books could be written about how people arrange
their living spaces in order to deal with certain aspects of their
relationships. Family therapists who conduct some of their
sessions in people's homes know that fact is often stranger than
fiction. One encounters flats with walls erected to divide a

---

DIY EXERCISE: NO SEX PLEASE, WE'RE MARRIED

---

Some couples feel they need to get closer but don't quite
know how to do it. Closeness may mean sex and that may have
become too mechanical. This exercise is a deliberate attempt
to look at each other in a new light – without slipping into
familiar sex routines. In fact if this exercise results in sex you
must be doing something wrong.

- Both set a whole weekend aside.
- Buy some (washable) body paint.
- Book into a hotel or, if financially stretched, book your own
  home – but exclude all familiar disturbances (put on the
  telephone answering machine, draw the curtains, don't
  answer the doorbell, etc).
- Divide the weekend into four body-painting sessions, lasting
  approximately three hours each.
- Take off any clothes you want to take off.
- Take it in turns to paint each other – skin only.
- Talk about how you see each other and why you have
  painted your partner in that particular way – if you want to.
- Stop after three hours and have a bath (but not together!).
- Take an hour on Sunday night, perhaps over a meal or a
  quiet drink, and discuss whether you have seen or
  experienced something new.
- Repeat if necessary.

living room; with two separate doors and mini-corridors leading to the same kitchen, which has double sets of machines and
utensils, one lot strictly for him and one for her. One sees
open-plan arrangements in flats with no curtains and the
couple complain that they have no privacy because 'everybody
can see what we do'.

And there are those large houses, with signs of eternal
building work everywhere, with only two floors converted and
lived in and the other three floors covered with rubble and
dust sheets. It is then no surprise to find that one of the
partners inhabits the top (usually the man) and one the base-

ment (usually the woman) – with a large buffer zone in be-tween. Some living arrangements may involve a third person, usually an adult child or a 'granny', who – starting off in the granny flat – is moved around from room to room, often resulting in one of the partners taking up full occupancy in the little flat.

It is quite possible for couples to live physically and emotion-ally separate lives under the same roof. In such 'marriages of convenience' they simply co-exist, with little interest in the other person, and this shows itself in many areas – not only the spatial arrangements but also the lack of physical contact. Again, this may suit both partners – or it may not. Often certain routines set in and people think they can no longer get any pleasure from one another. Not all is lost when partners have become bored with sex: there are ways of rediscovering one another . . .

Some relationships seem to be beyond help, as both part-ners feel they are in a prison. Often it is very difficult to determine who the jailer is and who the prisoner is – and it depends very much on one's perspective. The roles are quite often interchangeable. People can escape from a real or imagined 'prison marriage' by quite different routes.

## MID-LIFE ESCAPADES

Mid-life is traditionally the time for affairs. But this doesn't always involve falling in love with another man or woman. Other sorts of affairs can be equally powerful. For example, there are those men and women who start having passionate affairs with the bottle and drink themselves into oblivion. Often the alcohol replaces the partner and the relationship can be equally intense – alternately loving and cursing the bottle, being relieved and made sick by it. Alcoholism destroys most families. It is as if a new member has joined the family, and vain efforts are made to compete with this new arrival and its disastrous grip. There is much more to be said about why people drink and how the family can deal with it – but unfortu-nately space does not permit.

Another common mid-life affair is with work. When grown men or women marry their jobs it often spells trouble. The work setting can become a substitute for the family, where he can be the paternalistic father he feels he is not allowed to be at home. Or where she, undermined and taken for granted at home, can feel competent and professional. Many women see work as the major source of their self-esteem and it is therefore no surprise when, once the children have left home, they spend more and more time and energy on their jobs, much to the annoyance of their husbands. Just when the husband has resolved to take life a bit easier and spend more time at home with his wife, she decides she wants to develop her career or even start a new one.

But let us now concentrate on the most common of all mid-life escapades: affairs of the heart, fatal or liberating attractions to another person of the same or opposite sex. Mid-life, often referred to as 'second adolescence', affects both men and women. Halfway through life people naturally want to take stock. Looking to the past and future, the questions arise:

– What have I done? And what haven't I done?
– Am I happy with my lot? Do I need to change?
– Shall I go it alone or involve my family?
– What lies ahead?
– How can I use the next few years to fulfil some of my ambitions?

The fear that time is running out and the realization that the process of ageing has started can drive both men and women into last-minute panics. The forms these take often seem ridiculous to onlookers. When men and women in their fifties and sixties behave as if they were a fraction of their biological age, they can present a sad sight. Deluding themselves that they are now freer and more liberated than ever before, they deny the limitations of their bodies. Men camouflage their middle-age spread behind pretty blondes or brunettes half their age and a quarter their size, proving to themselves (and nobody else) that they can still attract desirable women.

When facing the realities of their bodies, men and women

alike have different parts of their anatomies lifted, expanded or reduced, in a vain attempt to gain a few extra minutes of youth. Driving their not-so-young bodies through the latest toning machines and exercise routines, they keep looking for someone richer, more beautiful, sexier, blonder, darker, taller, slimmer, shorter, brighter or dimmer. But, whilst the grass seems greener on the other side, once you're there you soon discover that it might in fact have been greener where you came from.

Yet not all men or women go crazy in middle age. So who are the most likely candidates?

*Alan and Ianthe had been childhood sweethearts. In love since their early teens, they started living together when they were both seventeen and their first baby was born just a year later. Another three babies later they were in their mid-twenties and by the time the last child had left home they had entered their forties. Both had just about survived the daily struggles of bringing up a largish family but this had not been without considerable sacrifices. Ianthe regretted most that she had never gone to college and Alan felt that he had missed out on the sort of things his mates at school had always boasted about: pubs, football and girls.*

*Alan and Ianthe gave each other permission to have an 'open' relationship. Ianthe enrolled in a course at a college and Alan made contact with his old mates. A few months later he seemed totally changed: he sported the latest haircut, invested in fashionable clothes and aftershave and looked – or at least acted – as if he were in his late teens. He went to the pub every night, spent days away from home at marathon parties, experimented with drugs and boasted to his mates about his latest one-night stand. Ianthe meanwhile enjoyed her studies and quickly made a number of good friends, almost all of them at least half her age. She felt flattered that they liked her and formed a strong relationship with a twenty-five-year-old student who became her lover.*

*A few months passed and Alan got tired of his new lifestyle. He started missing Ianthe whom he hardly saw. He knew about her relationship and it began to bother him. It was just then that Alan and Ianthe became grandparents, the first time round, at the tender age of forty-three. This event made them closer for a few weeks. Alan told Ianthe that it made him feel really old and she replied that she felt like the youngest grandmother on earth.*

What will happen to Alan and Ianthe's relationship is still uncertain at this point. It is as unpredictable as it is for the many other couples who open up their relationships in the middle of their lives. Doing so means taking a risk – whereas avoiding the risk can lead to a lifetime of regrets about missed opportunities. When men or women feel that, because of family circumstances, they were forced to lead a life that wasn't really what they wanted, they will wish to experiment later on in life.

For example, many people who feel that they were forced into a marriage because of parental pressure, will want to test whether life might have been different if they had not given in to that pressure. For some, the experiment shows that what one is used to is the best one can expect – but that there might be room for improvement: it is never too late. For others, it proves that radical change is required – and this means permanent separation.

This can take the form of living alone, an option that women tend to be more interested in, particularly after years of being a glorified though unappreciated housewife. Others – more frequently men – can only see themselves in another relationship. Some people compromise by going into increasingly popular part-time relationships, with both partners living in their separate flats and getting together if and when they feel like it.

In order to force a separation, some men and women may go as far as 'prescribing' affairs for their partners – in the hope that this might get rid of them, or that it will make them more appreciative of what they have got. Plenty of relationships are strengthened by an affair because the long-term relationship can then be evaluated in relation to another man or woman. However, in our officially monogamous culture, most affairs appear to be unmitigated disasters and are used in relationship

DIY EXERCISE: MAPPING YOUR LIFE

- Sometimes it can be helpful to take a new look to evaluate who and what is important in one's life.
- Take a largish piece of paper and draw a big circle covering most of it: this circle stands for your life and family now.
- Draw some smaller circles to represent all the other people who are important to you – family members, friends etc.
- Initial each circle so that you can identify it.
- People can be inside or outside the large circle, touching, overlapping or far apart. They can be large or small, depending on how important they are to you. They can be alive or not.
- Now put yourself in.
- Also put in other important areas of your life – work, hobbies, religion, garden, pets or whatever.
- Take about 5 minutes to do this drawing. Then step back, have a look at it, and ask yourself:
  – Does your life look full or empty?
  – What do you make of how you have drawn the circles?
  – What about the spaces between people? Are the circles too overcrowded?
  – Is there enough room for your interests?
  – Is there anybody you did not want to put on the map?
  – Does anything strike you about the sizes of the circles?
  – Do you like this picture?
  – Is there any room for change?
  – How would you like it to be different?
- Now think what you would like this picture to look like:
  – Which circles should get bigger?
  – Which smaller?
  – Is there any room for new circles, etc?
- What would change if you separated from your partner?
- You can now play around with the circles, make them bigger or smaller and see how, if one gets smaller, there may suddenly be additional space – or how life gets too empty.

Mapping out your life in this way can help you think about the implications of change and plan what step to take next.

battles for years afterwards. When divorce proceedings are instigated, affairs are likely to be dragged up from the past and used as evidence of the partner's infidelity, be it 'prescribed' or spontaneous. Looking for the guilty party may at times be appropriate, but on the whole it takes two to make or break a marriage.

## SEPARATION AND DIVORCE

The final days of marriages and other long-term relationships are often littered with arguments, as if to prove that there is no hope whatsoever. The more arguments rage, the more justification there seems to be for separating. Unfortunately children and other more or less innocent bystanders often get caught up in this domestic warfare. Controlling one's arguments does not stop divorce proceedings – it just makes life more bearable in the interim, which may be years. Keeping a record of arguments, using the exercise opposite, is one way of decreasing and controlling them.

Legal divorce is one thing, emotional divorce another. When two ex-partners continue to argue whenever they meet, or when they refuse to speak to one another, they are still emotionally involved. The anger of one or both ex-partners keeps them tied together. Legal divorces are fairly quick compared with the majority of emotional ones.

### Divorcing the in-laws

Strong family connections across the generations often make it difficult to cut all ties. 'Divorcing the in-laws' can be a very lengthy process, particularly if one is indebted to them for help in the past. They can also be used as go-betweens by one or both partners to prolong the agony.

One of the most difficult issues for step-families is to accept that parts of the old family need to be involved with the new. This does not only apply to ex-partners but also to grandparents. The wish to exclude the past is very understandable but, whilst it is possible to divorce one's wife, it is impossible, to date, for grandchildren to be divorced from their grand-

DIY EXERCISE: KEEPING AN ARGUMENT DIARY

This involves charting arguments over the course of a week
and can be done by one person or more. The two 'arguers'
should keep separate diaries.
- Prepare a column (or page) for each day and record:
  - when the argument happened
  - who or what, in your view, triggered it
  - what it was apparently about
  - who was present
  - where it took place
  - how long it lasted
  - how it stopped.
- Do this for a whole week. At the end of this time, examine
  your findings, first by yourself and then with the other party.
- See whether there is a pattern to your arguments. For
  example:
  - Is there a specific time or day when they are more likely to
    happen? A specific place? A specific 'audience'?
  - What is the most likely way of stopping an argument?
Answering these questions should help you predict how, when
and where arguments are likely to take place. This exercise
also shows which of your own strategies are likely to stop an
argument – and which are bound to fail. This allows you to
take evasive action, such as using humour or distraction, or
simply absenting yourself for a given time.
- Knowing how, when and where arguments start makes it
  possible to stop them – or to have them in private. Now
  choose one predictable argument and see whether you can
  make it run a different course. For example, you can
  change:
  - where you are going to have the argument (e.g. without
    the children present, or in the bathroom instead of the
    bedroom)
  - when you are going to have it (after dinner, before the in-
    laws arrive)
  - how you have it (standing up, lying down, from a distance)
  - how you resolve it (e.g. with humour, or after a set time
    limit)

parents. This, however, is only a legal point. In practice, unfortunately, grandparents are frequently punished by the ex-son- or ex-daughter-in-law and any contact is forbidden. The grandchildren may feel equally penalized by these actions and deprived of what may already be a very important relationship.

However children are often very fond of their grandparents, uncles and aunts, irrespective of whether or not they happen to be related to the so-called 'guilty party'. It is important for children not to lose contact with the in-laws, as the loss of home stability is usually devastating enough. If this is coupled with further loss of contact with people close to them the damage is multiplied. If parents and in-laws can bear this in mind then it may be possible to preserve some continuity for the children at a time of significant change.

## STEP-FAMILIES

When two partners get married for the first time to one another, two families are joined together. As we have seen, this is a complex enough enterprise. Multiply this by two or more and you have a situation in which two partners, both of them previously divorced and with children, get remarried: effectively this means that four or more families have to establish a new *modus vivendi* – and this takes some time and a lot of effort.

Families that form through remarriage have to cope with different issues from those each partner may have encountered in their previous family lives. When children are involved it requires, for example, giving up the notion of a traditional nuclear family, as it is usually not possible or advisable to refuse access to the biological parents. Given that most children continue to have strong attachments to both their parents, divorce or not, the influence of the absent parent becomes a strong dynamic in the step-family's life. One of the tasks step-families are faced with is finding appropriate ways of sharing the responsibilities of bringing up the children. This not only involves negotiation between parent and step-parent, but also needs to take into account the role of the absent parent.

---

DIY EXERCISE: MAKING IT EASIER FOR THE CHILDREN

---

Here are some suggestions which have proved helpful to some families. They may apply to yours.

- If children have a good relationship with their other parent then making it easy for them to have contact, within the framework of existing legal agreements, is beneficial to them.
- Consider whether or not to question children as to why they want to see your ex-partner. Children usually have divided loyalties. They probably know that you do not want them to go and they may get caught in a loyalty conflict: if they do go they fear that they are letting you down; if they don't they fear letting their other parent down.
- Consider whether, given your children's ages, it is appropriate for them to help decide on custody issues, access arrangements or remarriage.
- Consider whether it is wise to compete with the step-child's attachment to your partner.
- Consider whether it is wise to compete with the step-child's other parent.
- Question the assumption that women are always better parents and that all parental responsibilities should therefore be delegated to the step-mother: this could set her up to fail.
- Explore whether it is possible for you and your ex-spouse to take joint primary responsibility for bringing up your child(ren).
- Discuss the implications of this with your current partner.

*Rachel was nine years old when her parents divorced. Her mother Joan married Robert and the new family were full of hope for a bright new future. Robert had two children from his first marriage who came to stay every other weekend. Joan tried to be extra nice to them as she wanted to have a good relationship with them from the very beginning.*

*After an initial 'honeymoon period', her step-children started testing her by refusing to do any of the household chores. Then all hell broke loose when Joan called them 'spoilt brats'. Robert defended his children and asked his new wife not to get involved in their upbringing and not to 'compete' with their birth mother. Joan felt excluded and angry.*

*The situation was further complicated when Rachel's father was granted regular access to see his daughter. Whenever she stayed with him he spent a lot of time criticizing Rachel's mother for having left him. To make things worse, Rachel did not like her father's girlfriend, particularly since she joined him in his criticisms of Rachel's mother – even though she had never met her. On her return, Rachel would tell her mother about what happened and then it was Robert's turn to run down Rachel's father.*

*Whenever Rachel's mother asked Robert to stop, he would see this as a sign that she was still attached to her ex-husband and this would then trigger a massive row. Rachel very quickly learned not to tell either her father or her mother what went on in the other one's house. She became very secretive and her mother often found her crying in her room. Rachel would not say what it was about.*

It is often the children who pay the price for unresolved issues between their separated parents. The parents are not always aware of how much their children's divided loyalties force them to be silent or start lying.

No child can be expected to adopt the parent's new partner as another parent straight away. This does not stop some children from professing 'instant love' and calling Mother's new partner 'Daddy' – a person who was a total stranger only two months ago. Children do this to please their parent or perhaps in desperation to replace a lost or dead parent. New families need to be given time to develop naturally. Step-parents and step-children can then form a relationship which feels right for all concerned, be that as friends, siblings, aunt and niece or, indeed, parent and child.

## Chapter 9

# The family in illness and death

IN THIS CHAPTER WE LOOK AT:

•

THE IMPACT OF SUDDEN ILLNESS ON THE
FAMILY

•

CHRONIC ILLNESS AND ITS EFFECTS ON
RELATIONSHIPS

•

HOW FAMILIES COPE WITH AGEING AND
DYING

•

LIFE-THREATENING ILLNESS AND DEATH

•

FAMILY LIFE AFTER SOMEONE HAS DIED

Serious illness and death are realities in all families. Yet Western society, with its ever-proliferating industry aimed at artificially postponing ageing, seems to deny the very existence of death. We continually try to prolong life by various means, even deep-freezing the dead (or just their brains) for some glorious resurrection in centuries to come. Care of the terminally ill is farmed out to specialist centres, far removed from the family. Even though most people would like to die at home, few have their wish granted.

Serious illness and death have major effects on the family, as when another family member develops related symptoms.

However, because of our collective denial, these are often not recognized. Serious illness requires a readjustment of the family structure, at least temporarily. Different family members find themselves in new roles, forced to solve unfamiliar problems. Having to hide the fact that they are over-stretched, of having to 'cope' without showing grief, sooner or later takes its toll.

How families cope with serious illness varies a great deal, according to the nature of the illness, whether its onset is sudden or gradual, expected or unexpected, and also how life-threatening it is. In addition there may be other factors which determine the family's response: previous experience with illness and loss; the timing of the illness in relation to the different family members' development; the position and role of the ill or dying member within the family; and the family's external support network.

## THE IMPACT OF SUDDEN ILLNESS ON THE FAMILY

Illness challenges the family's equilibrium: when one person is suddenly not functioning well then the overall functioning of the family machinery may be seriously disturbed or even come to a standstill.

> *Charles Percy was only forty-nine when he suffered his first heart attack – out of the blue. The whole family was in shock: would he survive? As the family sat in the intensive care unit of the district hospital, waiting anxiously for more news from the medical team, each member was preoccupied with their own worries about the immediate future.*
>
> *Mrs Percy could not help thinking about the big family row that had occurred literally one hour before her husband had collapsed. She felt guilty. She also felt worried about her eleven-year-old daughter Angela who seemed so obviously distressed by the thought that her father might die. Mrs Percy comforted her daughter but noticed that this left her teenage son Gregory all by himself. What was he thinking about? Was he worried about the financial implications? Mrs Percy suddenly panicked,*

*visualizing her husband, bed-ridden and chronically disabled,*
*with two needy and hungry children.*

Illnesses with a sudden onset require families to mobilize their crisis management skills quickly. How they adapt to the often unexpected and dramatic changes varies. At one extreme, some families continue to function as if nothing had happened. Illness and its effects are denied and the families never talk about it openly. Other families may be paralysed for months, with various members developing physical or psychological symptoms.

However the majority of families fall somewhere between these two extremes and somehow manage to establish a new equilibrium. This may require the oldest son to step into Dad's shoes temporarily and carry out certain tasks in the home. Mother has to take care of some family affairs that Father used to manage and, as Mother is doing extra work, her daughter will be required to take over some of her usual functions. Members of the extended family may volunteer their help and, bit by bit, the family establishes its new rhythm.

*Mr Percy made a good recovery and was discharged from hospital three weeks later. He had heard about how well everyone had worked together and was now able to see for himself. The doctors had prescribed a lot of rest and 'taking things easy'. His family treated him as if he were an invalid. He did not mind this initially, but soon he did not like it at all. After all, prior to his illness, he had been very fit and active.*

*He was pleased that the family had been able to cope without him, but he now also felt irritated by it. His son behaved as if he were the head of the family, his wife seemed to handle all the money matters (something about which she had pleaded total ignorance until the day he fell ill), and their daughter, highly irresponsible in the past, was doing many of the chores in the house that she had so persistently refused to do. And there was his mother-in-law, successfully banned from the house for years, making daily visits to prepare the meals. Where did this leave him? Was there anything left for him to do? Mr Percy decided to get well immediately to take over his familiar role in the home. Ten days later he suffered another heart attack.*

When a family member has been away for a while because of illness then the family needs to reallocate roles – temporarily. Once the convalescent returns to the home the family has to readjust. This is not always easy as some members, often to their surprise, will have found life easier without the ill member.

In the Percy family, which followed traditional gender roles before Father's illness, his prolonged absence forced everyone to take on new functions. There were therefore mixed responses to his return: his own status had diminished, whereas his wife's competence had been enhanced.

For a father to discover that the family machinery is ticking over without him may be depressing. It can seriously dent his self-esteem as he and other family members fluctuate between accepting and denying the illness and the limitations it causes for him.

Spending all day at home with his wife may be a novelty at first, but it can soon become problematic as too much exposure leads to conflicts. As the father has nothing much to do at

---

DIY EXERCISE: FACING ILLNESS
-------------------

Partners faced with an ill but previously well-functioning adult may find it helpful to consider the following:
• Listen to medical advice about what can and cannot be done.
• Discuss the advice and tell everyone in the household.
• Consider what role changes need to be made and for how long.
• Review the arrangements regularly, e.g. once a week, to allow for flexible responses to changing circumstances.
• Think of which jobs could be handed back to the ill person and at what point.
• Discuss with the ill person what changes need to be made so that relapse becomes less likely.
• Discuss this openly with everyone in the household.
• Remember that some jobs can be done from a resting position.
• When the ill person becomes depressed, don't just try to cheer him or her up or say 'Pull yourself together'. Find out through discussion what the issues are.

home, he may criticize his wife or accuse her of fussing too much over him. Sudden and unexpected illness always makes a lot of demands and the family needs to show flexibility to adapt.

Most people want to recover and get little satisfaction out of remaining in the invalid position. Some are too quick and risk a relapse because they find it unbearable to be seen as old or unfit: this makes a relapse more likely. On the other hand there are some people who develop a taste for illness and get addicted to some of its benefits. They can become chronically ill.

## CHRONIC ILLNESS AND ITS EFFECTS ON RELATIONSHIPS

Some chronic illness is serious because the sufferer is physically or psychologically incapacitated, as in the case of a child with cerebral palsy, an adult with multiple sclerosis, or a schizophrenic who is repeatedly admitted to mental hospital. Other chronic illness is, medically speaking, less serious but can still be fairly incapacitating. In many cases such illness becomes a way of relating to others and a part of the family fabric.

### Family headaches

*Ben, in his forties and married with three teenage children, had a long history of headaches. He had consulted a number of doctors and other specialists, but as nobody could find any physical reason for his symptoms they were labelled 'psychosomatic'. His wife and children had come to live with these headaches which would happen at random, at least once a month, and last for two or three days. During these spells Ben would have to withdraw to his study and remain isolated from the rest of the family.*

Some headaches – and other similar symptoms, such as abdominal pain, backache, etc – become part of family life. Everyone respects them; they change what goes on; they can be irritating; and at times they can be welcome companions. Calling certain aches and pains 'psychosomatic' does not imply that people are faking them: the pain is entirely real and the sufferers feel unable to control it. There may even be some physical evidence of illness or injury to 'explain' why it hurts in a particular part of the body – and not somewhere else. At other times the physical pain may be symbolic of some other stress.

*Ben was eventually referred to a family therapist. He decided to go without his family first and the therapist encouraged Ben to draw his family tree so that they could both search for clues in the past. It had never struck Ben how many of his family had suffered from pains in or around the head.*

*There was his mother who was a migraine sufferer and whose*
*symptoms had got much worse ten years ago, shortly after his*
*father's death from a stroke. Going back one generation, his*
*attention was drawn to his maternal grandmother who had*
*often been referred to as 'not being quite right in the head'. In*
*fact she had suffered from depression for many years and had*
*been admitted on a few occasions to a mental hospital. Further*
*probing revealed that Ben's twin brother had died a few days*
*after birth from hydrocephalus. Ben was quite shocked by this,*
*as he had not thought about it at all for many years.*

In some families, who have been through very painful experiences way back, any distress gets channelled through specific organs – the head, the heart, the back, the abdomen, etc. The physical symptoms a person experiences may point towards painful family issues, perhaps too painful to be put into words. The symptom is then the only way in which that issue lives on.

In Ben's case three generations had afflictions that, in one way or another, concerned the head. Is it any surprise then that he experienced distress in that particular region of his body? The head had become the family stress organ. The headaches might also have been serving as a reminder of some of the tragedies that had befallen his family. Further inquiry can clarify what these were.

Family therapists believe that some headaches and other pains can be cured when the sufferer connects current symptoms with past relevant events: discussing these openly and grieving appropriately makes the physical pain redundant.

*Ben felt both better and worse for having made these*
*connections. Almost unbearable sadness had replaced some of*
*the headaches. He had been to see his mother a few times and*
*they had both cried together about the tragic losses. His*
*headaches became less frequent.*

*Ben was encouraged to bring his family to the next therapy*
*session. Then, much to his irritation, he found the therapist*
*inquiring about the positive benefits his headaches had – for*
*Ben himself and for the various family members. His children*
*were quick to point out that it gave their father an excuse to*

*withdraw and have more space. They themselves did not mind, as they felt there was more freedom and only 'one boss' – their mother. She, in turn, seemed to have got used to the situation and she also stated that Ben's regular withdrawal gave her more space and time for herself – something she welcomed.*

---

DIY EXERCISE: FIGHTING FAMILY HEADACHES AND
OTHER PAINS

---

Consider whether there is someone in your family who is frequently or chronically ill where you suspect there is a strong psychological component.

- First look at the family pattern (draw a family tree, see page 15):
  - Who else had pains or illnesses in similar parts of the body?
  - At what age did this ailment develop?
  - What did/do people think this was to do with?
  - What was /is the effect of the illness on the various family members?
- Now look at the currently ill person:
  - What are the positive effects of the illness on the various family members and the family as a whole?
  - What would happen if the illness suddenly stopped?
  - What would be the disadvantages?
- Think about what might happen if you were to discuss your findings openly with the sufferer and/or the family as a whole. Before doing so, evaluate the risks. Could it cause major conflicts? How can you raise the subject tactfully and sensitively?

---

Illness is therefore not always an unwelcome visitor; indeed it can become a valued family friend. If Ben's headaches disappear altogether, the family will need to discuss openly how people can ask for time and space for themselves, without having to be ill. The pain of a physical symptom can sometimes seem preferable to having to confront this sort of issue.

**Chronic illness 'time bombs'**
Many chronic illnesses are serious and irreversible. Some of these illnesses are stable, others get progressively worse, and there are conditions which fluctuate. Living with a chronically ill person requires the family to devise a *modus vivendi*, based on the course of the illness. For many this is a rewarding task, but for some it becomes an endless ordeal.

Children born with disabilities, or those diagnosed as suffering from a serious though not fatal illness later in their childhood, tend to become quite special to their parents. This can lead to protective attitudes which may seem 'over-protective' to outsiders. It is, of course, understandable that the initial parental reaction to a diagnosis of, say, diabetes or epilepsy will be one of shock and a wish to shield the vulnerable child from all potential dangers. However the more the family protects the ill or disabled child, the less independent he or she will become. There are quite a number of 'children' in their twenties who have a localized disability, but who are treated as if they were totally physically and mentally handicapped, functioning like a three-year-old in an adult body.

Getting the balance right is, as usual, not easy and as children grow older their management needs to reflect this. Diabetic children, for example, may be very compliant with their treatment when they are younger and the illness can be well contained. But in adolescence, both the teenager and the diabetes can get totally out of control, with potentially life-threatening results. The family may feel it is sitting on a time bomb when the teenager starts threatening to use the illness as a way of blackmailing the parents.

It is not uncommon to use illness as a tool to get at others. A lot of repetitive self-harming behaviour, such as overdosing, contains elements of an attack on one's family. When words fail, self-destruction sends a very concrete message to those one loves and hates. Every further self-harming attempt makes it more difficult to reopen the channels of communication. Abnormal illness behaviour is a way of tying people down.

**The illness bond: in sickness and in health . . .**
*Mary had always been the sick one, the weak one, the one who*

*could never cope. Now, in her late thirties, it seemed that she
had been groomed for that role in her own family, with a mother
whose survival strategy had been to take to her bed at the
slightest sign of stress. This 'worked' in that her demanding
husband left her in peace and turned instead to their oldest
daughter Imogen for support in the household. She had become
substitute mother, partner and grandmother all rolled into one.*

*When Imogen left home at sixteen it seemed to be Mary's
turn. But Mary, then in her early teens, had already learned
that keeping a low profile in the family had its advantages. She
developed abdominal pains and sickness. Her younger sister
Jenny took over the household jobs. Like her mother, Mary had
developed a self-protective surface layer of 'illness', and nobody
was surprised when she married Bill, a psychiatric nurse.*

*Mary became Bill's second 'job' and he was constantly 'on
call' for his wife, at weekends and nights. For a while, the worse
she got the saner he felt. But then it all got too much: he had a
breakdown and was admitted to psychiatric hospital. On his
return he found that his wife had changed: she was now
prepared to look after him. She became his nurse, for a time . . .*

There are relationships in which one person is the 'patient'
and the other the 'nurse'. People stick with what is familiar and
this is often based on earlier experiences in their families of
origin. Many partners who become 'nurses' have themselves
learned that one way of conducting relationships is to look
after another person. This gives them a mission in life and also
a strong bond: ill people cannot be left by themselves. In the
unlikely event that the 'patient' recovers permanently, there is
always the possibility of another project: an elderly parent, a
child or another relative.

A considerable number of people working in the caring
professions have family backgrounds where looking after somebody else was an important part of their early lives. This may be
a better outlet than recreating the scenario in one's personal
life. For then the question arises, as it did for Mary and Bill,
whether anything other than the illness bond is keeping the
partners together. If the answer is 'no' then the couple may be
condemned to a never-ending relay race of nurse and patient.

## AGEING AND DYING

Old age is sometimes referred to as the 'third adolescence', with the old person hovering between dependence and independence, and having very different perspectives on life and those around them. Like adolescents, many old people do not fit easily into society. They seem to antagonize others and break rules, behaviour which may be attributed to senility or wisdom, often at random.

Modern Western society has little room for the elderly. Only two generations ago it was the rule rather than the exception for children to grow up in the same house as their grandparents. Many of those who did will have fond memories, not only of being spoilt with sweets, but of having a trusted ally in the home and someone who saw the world from a different angle. Close bonds between grandparents and grandchildren are now much rarer, as we tend to marginalize both our parents and our parents' parents.

With their failing health, their forgetfulness and their often unpredictable mood swings, old people often feel a nuisance to their children. If they were independent we would not mind having more contact with them. But, as they reach the end of their lives, they become more and more frail. When they fall ill it seems so much more dangerous, with the possibility of death so much nearer. This can lead to last efforts to unearth and tackle unfinished business.

*Mrs Coates, in her early eighties, was admitted to a psychogeriatric unit because of depression. At home she had acted in a very disturbed way for some months, accusing her husband, also in his eighties, of having an affair with the twenty-year-old cleaner. She was intensely suspicious of all his movements and whenever he was a few minutes late returning from the shops she would accuse him of having been to a brothel.*

*A psychiatrist was called in and diagnosed 'psychotic depression'. This brought their three children on to the scene. The oldest, a lawyer by profession, was very critical of the diagnosis. He had always been close to his mother and had believed for a long time that she had been treated badly by his father. He thought the accusations of infidelity were based on real evidence some years before and it was his father's continued cruelty towards his mother that made her feel it was happening now.*

*His sister, a teacher, took her father's side and joined with the psychiatrists in calling her mother 'mad', something she said she'd known for many years. Although she had her own teenage family to cope with, she decided to move in with her father to keep him company and look after him whilst her mother was in hospital. Her younger brother, a doctor, responded by saying that his sister only wanted to get her hands on the family money and possessions. He felt very aggrieved that his older brother, being the oldest boy, was due to inherit the family fortune and that now his sister seemed to be getting in on the act.*

*When the three of them met, ostensibly to discuss family matters, there was a physical confrontation between the two brothers in which the younger brother punched the older one. The last time the two of them had fought was forty years ago – in the sandpit.*

To some, impending death seems to offer a last chance to settle old scores. Final efforts are made to get wills changed, belongings transferred into different names and confessions extracted from half-demented elderly parents as to who has been the most caring of their children. Fights over money are often the visible manifestations of unfinished family business, hiding both frustration and rage over the love the children feel they never received and that no money in the world could ever buy. In the face of death, responsible adults can regress within minutes to child-like states, as if the last three or four decades had simply not happened. Being able to share the distress with family members, as well as talking about some of the good times long ago, are obvious ways of handling this difficult period – otherwise the distress will show up elsewhere.

**Relative symptoms**
When one person is seriously ill or dying, other family members may also develop symptoms. Often the prospect of death

is so devastating that people keep their grief to themselves. When worries cannot be openly expressed or shared then symptoms develop in another part of the family. Although this may be obvious to an outsider it is not usually apparent to the people inside the family.

*Mick, in his sixties, was dying from a brain tumour. He was divorced, with no children, but he had a brother, a sister, two nieces and an aunt. Closest to him was his brother Dick, two years his senior, who lived some 200 miles away. Dick made many journeys to see his brother in his final months. When back with his family he would complain about eye strain, difficulties in focusing and occasional headaches. His family put it down to the stress of commuting so much.*

*Everyone admired the way Dick coped with looking after his brother and it was only when Dick consulted a neurologist that his family became alarmed. He had been wondering whether he himself had a brain tumour, as he thought he had identical symptoms to his brother. Then his immediate family understood that Dick had become so burdened by his brother's illness that he felt he had to relieve some of his brother's symptoms by 'carrying' them himself. This was a signal for the rest of the family to help Dick by sharing the burden of looking after his brother.*

The way a family is affected by life-threatening illness and death depends on:

– the nature of the illness and death
– the timing of the death and how this relates to the various family members' ages and development
– the family's history of previous losses
– the position and role of the dying person
– the family's coping strategies which are affected by culture/ rituals
– the family's social support and network of friends

Clearly there are so many issues related to death, dying and bereavement that only some of them can be touched upon here. A sudden death, for example, through accident or

DIY EXERCISE: SPEAKING ABOUT THE UNSPEAKABLE

Death is one of the great taboo areas in our lives, yet talking about it is a vital part of coming to terms with this sort of loss. You may find it helpful to do some or all of the following:

• Name the illness and the cause of death.
• Share factual information openly: what happened before death, what people did and did not do when he or she was dying, the deceased person's last wishes, etc.
• Express thoughts and feelings freely.
• Cry when you feel like crying – don't cry if you don't feel like crying.
• Call on extra-familial sources of support (friends, religion, etc).
• Connect as much and as often as possible with sympathetic family members.
• View illness and death in context by looking at the family tree (see page 15) and discuss how your family has coped with death in the past.

suicide, will have a very different impact from a gradual, pre-dictable death after a slowly progressing terminal illness. In this case the family may be involved in the daily care of its dying member, with plenty of time to talk about the past, present and future. Relatives may oscillate in their feelings, from wishing the person dead, to feeling very guilty about such wishes, to wanting to do anything to make the person survive as long as possible. Again, if such mixed feelings – which are very com-mon – have to be kept secret, then the distress may show up in the form of a 'sympathetic illness'. Here the sufferer may develop symptoms not dissimilar to those of the dying person.

The dying person's age and position in the family will very much affect the family's responses. The more the family emo-tionally depends on the dying person, the more difficult it is to let go. Death at an older age is viewed as more acceptable, even though it is often not 'dignified' but the result of a chronic debilitating illness. Yet, however old the parent, the effects can be devastating and lead to serious depression, particularly when old business has been left unfinished. There is no more chance to forgive or be forgiven and the bereaved family members may be full of guilt and anger.

Perhaps life's worst tragedy is the death of a child. Since most people view children as extensions of themselves, representing many of their own hopes and aspirations, losing a child is devastating, and may have many long-term effects on the parental relationship and the siblings. Often there is a wish to replace a dead child, sometimes giving it the same name, so that it grows up with another identity belonging to the 'ghost'.

## LIFE AFTER DEATH

Death is a very private matter and this book does not attempt to give any facile advice on how to handle it. It is perhaps more helpful to think about life after death.

One does not have to be religious to believe in life after death. There is no doubt that many of those who have died can remain very much alive in people's memories. When we feel guilty about not having been caring enough towards one of our parents whilst they were still alive, we think about them as if they felt neglected now. But that makes no sense. They are dead and, unless we are spiritualists, we do not usually believe that the dead are with us and observe our actions. Some people think more about their parents and grandparents once they are dead than they ever did when they were alive. In our dreams we wake them up from the dead and then get haunted by the mistakes we made.

There are also those family members whom we cannot allow to die, whom we immortalize with pictures that stare at us day and night. Sometimes a dead person seems to come to life when a child, without knowing it, appears to impersonate a dead grandparent. Some families indirectly reinforce those of their children's traits which are reminiscent of the dead person. Such children can appear like ghosts themselves. With their stooped posture, shuffling gait and characteristic speech patterns they may fill the gap the dead grandparent has left.

DIY EXERCISE: HOW TO KILL A GHOST

Prolonged grief reactions may be partly due to an inability to 'let the dead person go'. Putting some flesh on the bones of the ghost may help to explain why he or she keeps haunting you, make the death a reality, and enable you finally to lay the person to rest.

• Discuss the dead person with people who knew him or her.
• Talk about the person's strengths and weaknesses.
• Remember times when the dead person made a fool of themselves – when s/he made people laugh.
• Get the facts about the person's death – what happened shortly before s/he died, at the time, and shortly afterwards.
• Visit the grave regularly if possible.
• Sometimes it can be helpful to write a letter to the dead person to clarify what one might want to tell him or her:
   – the good things he or she should know about
   – the bad things
   – the things one could never talk about when the person was alive.
• The next step could be to imagine how the dead person might respond, by writing an imaginary letter from the dead person to yourself or another family member.

Until the family can address their grief and associated feelings openly, this is done indirectly by somebody alive representing somebody dead. Dead family members who had not been allowed to die are usually either idealized or demonized. To allow them to die a natural death, they have to become ordinary people, with ordinary strengths and weaknesses.

Bereavement, though it is undoubtedly a difficult time, can have many positive effects on family relationships. Through shared grief people can get closer to one another, making connections that were not possible before. Bereavement enables family members not only to reminisce about good times in the past but also to think about how shared past and present grief can help to build new bridges in the future.

## Chapter 10

# Further help – the family as 'patient'

IN THIS CHAPTER WE LOOK AT:
•
WHO TO TURN TO FOR HELP
•
HOW FAMILY THERAPY WORKS
•
WHAT HAPPENS IN FAMILY THERAPY
•
THE DANGERS AND BENEFITS OF FAMILY THERAPY

When people face problems in their relationships or families they quite rightly start by trying to sort them out themselves. Self-help is the most natural response, and if that doesn't work most people have family or friends to turn to. There are times, however, when the family does not feel like a positive resource but, rather, an obstacle to change. In such situations, trying to involve the family can lead to more problems or make the problems worse instead of resolving them. Sometimes people are so stuck in their routines that they go round and round in circles, without any hope of moving on. This is the point when an outsider can help.

Why not ask a friend for help – someone who is more

objective? Indeed, why not? And this is often the first port of call. But, because of divided loyalties, friends may find it difficult to be as frank as a professional. They frequently get too involved and become part of the problem, unable to detach themselves from the family in trouble. After a while, being called repeatedly after midnight can become too much even for a best friend – and his or her family or partner. Everybody has their limit.

*Emily was eight when she became a real problem to her parents, Mr and Mrs Jones. She was cheeky and disrespectful and never did what her parents asked her. Some of the problems, her parents thought, were due to her having been partly brought up by her maternal grandparents.*

*Shortly after Emily's birth her parents had gone through a difficult patch and her mother moved back to her own parents for two years. During this time there was fairly limited contact between Emily and her father. Her grandmother took great care of her, as Emily's mother was depressed much of the time. A very special bond developed between Emily and her grandmother, and this continued when the parents got together again a few years later. Emily would stay with her grandparents every weekend and, as they lived only a block away, there was almost daily contact.*

*Emily remained Granny's favourite grandchild even though there was now a little brother, Alexander (aged five), and a sister, Tessa (aged three). Emily's behaviour had deteriorated ever since her brother's birth. When the parents had difficulties they had turned to their own parents for advice, but talking it over did not help and led to mutual blaming. When Emily started cutting up her mother's dresses and repeatedly flooding the bathroom the family decided they needed professional help. The parents were also concerned about the younger children's behaviour, as they seemed to copy Emily.*

## WHO DO YOU TURN TO FOR HELP?

When families are in distress and consider getting professional help they often do not know who to turn to. The general practitioner may be an obvious choice but whether one can trust him or her with one's family problems depends very much on one's relationship with the individual doctor. Some GPs, even though they may be referred to as 'family doctors', simply do not think of problems as being related to family issues. Brought up in a medical tradition, they look for some kind of disease or disorder inside their patient.

Such doctors may start by doing some tests to exclude the possibility of a physical cause for the patient's distress. The way the patient or family presents the problem to the doctor will to some extent affect his or her response. If Emily's mother, for example, asked about her perhaps being a 'hyperactive child' then this might lead to a line of inquiry focusing on her eating habits and possible food allergies, and consideration of diets and other related measures.

*In the event, Emily's mother told her sympathetic family doctor about Emily's recent behaviour. The doctor thought she should be referred to a child psychiatrist for an assessment.*

Where Emily – or any other child or adult – is referred depends partly on the doctor's familiarity with locally available resources and perhaps personal acquaintance with professionals. The doctor's own orientation and experience are also crucial: some doctors, when faced with the mother or father of a child, may have serious doubts as to who the 'patient' is. They may regard the child as relatively normal, and the parents as rather strange and much more in need of treatment than their offspring. But how can this be put to them? Parents rarely take kindly to the suggestion that it is they who need help, and not their children. This is why referring them for 'help as a family' is more acceptable than singling out an adult. But is this ethical? Are the children then being used as a way of getting help for the parents?

## WHAT SORT OF HELP?

Help comes in many different forms, some of which specifically address the person who has been 'identified' as the patient or problem, and some of which put the person in context and treat the family as 'the patient'. Broadly speaking, there are four distinct approaches to psychological problems. The first three all focus on the person who has – or is said to have – 'the problem'.

Firstly, there is the organic approach, where psychological symptoms or problems are seen as being the result of some physical cause, such as genetic and constitutional factors, biochemical disorder, injury, infection, tumour or allergies. The treatments prescribed are 'physical' and include medicines (e.g. anti-depressants, tranquillizers or hormone replacement), surgery, and even electro-shock treatment.

Secondly, there is the psychodynamic approach where psychological symptoms are seen as being connected with traumas early on in life. These 'talking therapies' aim to help the sufferer to re-address old conflicts, within the relationship that develops with the therapist.

Thirdly, there is the behavioural approach whereby psychological problems are seen as the result of 'wrong' learning – for instance 'learning' to be afraid of open spaces, spiders or over-close relationships. Behavioural therapy targets these fears and helps sufferers to unlearn what they have wrongly learned, with the help of a number of different techniques.

These rather diverse approaches have one thing in common: they all see the problem as being located *inside* the person and therefore apply the remedies solely to the sufferer.

The family approach differs from this, in that it sees problems as developing *between* people, in living contexts, such as the family or other important relationships. Even if one person appears to be more the cause than the rest of the family, everybody is still involved and therefore gets affected. This is why more than one person is included in the therapy: it is an *inter*-personal rather than an *intra*-personal approach.

Some family therapists believe that anyone's and everyone's

problems can be explained by blaming the entire family. This is, of course, nonsense. Problems almost always have a multitude of causes, some of them existing simultaneously. A depressed man, for example, may not only have cancer but also have suffered from depression for decades before he became physically ill. He may have been told by specialists that the 'old' depression was genetic and probably the result of some biochemical imbalance. In addition, our depressed man may have discovered in psychotherapy that he suffered many deprivations as a baby, which caused conflicts that had to be repressed and which only emerged later in life. And, to cap it all, our patient is also aware that he has wrongly learned to be afraid of social gatherings, a problem that has made him rather isolated. In other words, there are organic, psychodynamic and behavioural factors explaining his current (and past) depression. Why then prescribe family therapy for him?

Family therapy complements rather than competes with other approaches. If our depressed man has a family then his depression will affect them and their responses will in turn affect him. The family is involved with him and can therefore help him – and he may be able to help them to cope with him. Nobody in their right mind would argue that the family had caused the depression or, worse, the cancer. However problems and illnesses grow in living contexts and it is only common sense to involve those around – if the degree of suffering requires this and if the person and family want outside help.

## GETTING FAMILY THERAPY

So where does this leave Emily and her family in their quest for help? Finding a family therapist is not easy, as there are relatively few people officially known as family therapists. However there are many professionals from different disciplines who have been trained to work with families in a variety of settings. They include social workers, psychologists, GPs, psychiatrists, child psychotherapists, nurses, teachers and others. If a child is the major focus of the family's distress, then referral to a child guidance clinic (or a child and family psychiatry clinic) is often the best way of getting family therapy. At times a very medically oriented GP may need a lot of persuasion to make a referral. If this proves impossible then one can contact child mental health services or child guidance clinics directly, as many of them welcome self-referrals. Many social work departments also employ experienced family therapists.

If the major concern is over an adult family member then the options are more limited. The local psychiatric unit may have a family therapy team and there are a number of health centres and medical practices which offer family therapy on site. There are also several institutes, most of them private, that specialize in family therapy. And within the private sector, there are an increasing number of therapists who provide family therapy in their consulting rooms.

Unfortunately it is not easy to tell how reputable private institutes or therapists are. Although there are lists of registered family therapists and counsellors available, these provide

no guarantee of getting a good therapist. Word-of-mouth recommendation by a trusted professional is probably most likely to result in a good match between family and therapist.

### Who should go to family therapy?

*Emily was referred by the GP to their local child guidance clinic and they received a letter inviting 'the family' to attend. Mr and Mrs Jones wondered who should go. Would it not be better if only Emily's mother went first and explained what the problem was? Or should they both go?*

*Mrs Jones telephoned the clinic to inquire and was told that the parents should bring whoever they thought should come. Mrs Jones did not think this was much help and she discussed it further with her husband. Mr Jones started wondering if Emily's granny should attend the first meeting 'because she interferes with everything we do'. His wife did not like this comment. In the event they both agreed that they would bring all their children, but that they would have a 'private word' with the therapist beforehand to fill in some of the background.*

Some years ago, when family therapy was still in its infancy, family therapists used to insist on seeing 'the whole family'. What they meant by that was based much more on their definition of what constituted a family than on that of the people concerned. Some therapists required the attendance not only of the immediate family but also of all grandparents, uncles and aunts. If any of them could not or would not make it, the session was cancelled. On the whole, families don't like to be told who should or shouldn't come and there are certain members who would simply not dream of attending a family therapy session. Should the rest of the family be punished in such cases and not receive any help?

Nowadays many family therapists will invite 'the family' for the first session but agree to see whoever turns up. It is not uncommon for the number of clients attending the actual therapy sessions to increase over time from one person to as many as six or ten, including members of the extended family or relevant others. Given that different cultures – and different families – have widely differing ideas of what constitutes 'the family', it is surely right to respect the decisions of the family and its individual members.

Even if only one person attends the first family therapy session this can still be useful. The job of the family therapist is then to find out why only one – two or three – people have turned up. How the family and its members arrived at that decision is often a good indication of issues inside the family. If, for example, a father does not want to come to therapy sessions because he regards bringing up the children as his wife's job, then this already gives us a glimpse of some of the issues this family might be struggling with.

If both grandparents attend the first session this might say something about their role in the family. If they do not come, as in the case of Emily's family, then asking how the decision was made may reveal some of the underlying family dynamics (for instance that the father believes the maternal grandmother to be 'interfering').

But would the family actually let on about this conversation in front of a total stranger? Perhaps not in the first session. However, after a while, most family members realize that it is a waste of time to conceal certain issues from the therapist.

**What happens in family therapy?**
It is the therapist's job to tune into the family and build up a trusting relationship with them as quickly as possible, so that they feel able to talk about sensitive issues. This task is not made any easier by some of the modern technology often found in family therapy clinics, which initially makes families feel as if they were in a goldfish bowl. Commonly used items of equipment include a video camera, a microphone and a one-way mirror with a team of professionals hidden behind it, able to see and hear what goes on in the therapy room, but themselves invisible. How could anybody possibly be relaxed enough in such an environment to talk about their innermost fears and worries?

Many families feel quite ill at ease when first told about the set-up of the therapy room. The therapist will be at pains to explain the reason for this: namely that it is useful to have more than one pair of ears and eyes to observe what goes on and that this can provide another perspective which may be helpful to the family. The therapist will go on to explain that members of the team may wish to share their ideas, sometimes with the therapist and sometimes with the family. This will be done by the therapist leaving the room and talking to the team behind the one-way screen. Sometimes members of the team come into the therapy room and talk to the therapist in front of the family. In addition, the therapist may ask the family for permission to make a videotape of the session so that the team can study it afterwards to see whether there are any additional observations that might have been missed. Again, it is stressed that this is for the benefit of the family.

Family therapy has broken many taboos. It has been argued that the arrival of the one-way screen has been as significant as the invention of the telescope. Viewing the world differently makes it possible to think innovatively, and the one-way screen allows the therapeutic team to see the family in a more detached way. Moreover, videotaping family sessions and studying them afterwards allows the therapist to view things from a different perspective.

New perspectives produce new theories and one of the major discoveries resulting from the use of screen and video is how closely linked the apparently strange or 'crazy' behaviour of a person is with communication patterns within the family. Replaying the same videotape of a specific family interaction over and over, with the possibility of pausing and using slow motion, allows family therapists to study sequences in minute detail. This makes it possible to look at what precedes a specific behaviour or communication, how this affects other people in the room, and how their reaction in turn affects further communications. Sometimes the family will study a specific interaction on tape, together with the therapist, in order to see themselves from a bird's eye view. This can be very helpful to the families concerned.

Having described some of the technology that family therapists have grown fond of, it now needs to be said that most family therapy happens without one-way screens, teams of professionals or videos. In fact experienced family therapists will only occasionally resort to these techniques – usually when they feel stuck and want a 'second opinion'. That other perspective can be equally well provided by a consultant sitting in the room rather than being hidden away. One-way screens and video cameras are important for family therapists in training, but they are usually too labour-intensive to be used in the ongoing treatment of any one family, although they can be helpful from time to time.

For a considerable number of families these gadgets are more of a hindrance than a help, and a sensitive therapist will adjust to the needs of the particular family.

> *The Jones family entered the room and did not know where to sit. The therapist left it to them to decide and Emily found herself sandwiched between her parents, with her younger siblings running riot in another part of the room. The parents looked helplessly at the therapist. He encouraged them to take their time and to settle the children.*
>
> *Mother looked at Father; Father looked at Mother and said, 'You do it.' She got up and begged her children to sit down next to the parents. The father told his wife that she was too soft and that wasn't the way to get them to behave. She should tell them 'Once and for all, that they've got to do what you want them to do'. The mother replied that her husband should tell them to behave because they only ever listened to him. The children, pausing for a few moments in their loud and destructive play, soon increased their activities, ignoring any instructions their parents gave them.*

Family therapists are very keen to observe ordinary family interactions. Watching the parents settle their children can provide vital clues as to how the mother and father may or may not work together. This is why the therapist refuses to get drawn in – there is little point in him struggling to get the children under control. After all, he does not live with the family and part of his job is to help the parents find better ways of coping with everyday issues.

It may also be of interest to the therapist to note where Emily is sitting. This can, but need not necessarily be, symptomatic of her position in the family. It could be seen as a metaphor for the way she usually gets between her parents.

The therapist will frequently encourage the family members to 'enact' problems in the consulting room. This allows him or her to observe how the parents disqualify one another, and what happens when the children take no notice of their parents.

*It took Mr and Mrs Jones some ten minutes to calm down their two younger children, with the therapist highlighting how each parent seemed to have a different approach with regard to the best way of settling the children. Once the parents co-ordinated their efforts and Father got up from his chair as well, the younger children responded.*

*Then it seemed to be Emily's turn to play up: she got up and left the room. The parents looked at the therapist who again asked them to do whatever they thought they had to do to deal with the situation. Emily was recovered, after a considerable struggle, and another five minutes later everyone sat in their chairs. The session could begin.*

Begin? In fact the session was already in full flow. The therapist could now get straight into some of the issues – asking them whether 'this kind of battle for control' was a typical situation, whether they found this a problem and, if so, what they usually did to resolve it.

Despite the fact that most people would regard a consulting room as a very artificial setting, family chemistry is so strong that reactions take place irrespective of the context. The therapist makes possible and prolongs such interactions. This should enable the family to bring issues out into the open, so that everyone can think about how to resolve them.

Most family therapists find it safest to start with what the family sees as the problem rather than giving their own definition of the problem. For instance, if the therapist immediately comments on how the parents are 'not getting their act together' and hints that this has to do with their marital relationship, he might well be going too far too quickly – even if what he says happens to be true. This family has not come for therapy to resolve marital difficulties – at least not yet. If they want to tackle their own relationship then the therapist has to wait until they are ready – otherwise the family will not return for follow-up visits.

Focusing on the presenting problem means finding out when it happens, how often, where, what precedes it, what the 'rewards' for the problematic behaviour are and how these maintain the problem(s). In short, many of the self-help DIY exercises described in this book are well-known family therapy techniques – with the one difference that they are introduced or prescribed by the therapist.

What, then, can a therapist do that the family cannot do themselves? The therapist can get the family to take a new look at themselves in the way that only an outsider can. He or she can then, together with the family, discuss new ways forward. In this way the various family members become 'co-therapists'.

*By the end of the first session Mr and Mrs Jones felt that they had had a fairly good hearing. They had been able to explain their difficulties with Emily. Emily had told them that her grandparents understood her better and that her parents seemed to prefer her brother and sister. Her little sister had thrown a tantrum in the middle of the session because she was clearly not getting enough attention. The parents both got caught up in trying to control her, constantly undermining one another. During this struggle Emily played with her brother, keeping him occupied. The parents did not seem to notice this demonstration of Emily's competence but turned on her the moment her little sister was quiet, reciting a catalogue of her misdeeds.*

A whole string of issues can often emerge in the first session and the therapist has to work out a focus, together with the family. It is a bit like dealing with the different layers of an onion: one has to peel away the top layer before one can see the next – and there are many layers before one gets to the core. The top layer in family therapy is often the symptom and concentrating on this – making it better, as it were – is the first step. Once some success is achieved, the family will have some confidence in the therapist and allow him or her to look at what is underneath.

*At the end of the first session the therapist gave the family some homework: to compile, over a period of two weeks, two diaries, one for Emily's good behaviours and one for her problem ones. Emily was to participate in this and fill it in at the end of every day, in consultation with her parents.*

*A fortnight later, to their surprise, the parents reported that there had been a remarkable improvement. The only difficult times they could remember had been on the weekends, just after returning from her grandparents on both Sunday afternoons. The parents also reported that their younger children's behaviour had got worse.*

Diaries often have an immediate effect: the process of observation changes what is being observed. By being involved in compiling the diary Emily became more aware of what she was doing. Moreover, knowing that her behaviour was being scrutinized, she could not behave in the same way. It also meant that her parents had more and different contact with her: for instance having a day's review every evening when filling in the diary.

This tends to alter the balance at home and it is no surprise to the family therapist that if one person gets better, another gets worse. Further sessions with the family will address this issue and help the parents to think of ways in which they can balance more fairly the positive attention they give each child. The other piece of information emerging from the diary was Emily's unsettled behaviour following her weekend stay with her grandparents.

*The second and third family therapy session focused on how the parents could give reasonably equal amounts of positive attention to all three children. Some changes had been made by the family and things seemed to be fine for most of the week. However there still remained the difficult time on Sundays. At this point Mr and Mrs Jones suggested that the grandparents should come to the next family meeting.*

*The fourth session was attended by Mr Jones, Mrs Jones and both her parents. After a long discussion Emily's parents decided not to bring the children but to have them looked after by a friend. The session was very emotional, with the grandparents accusing Mrs Jones of neglecting Emily. Mr Jones defended his wife, the grandmother attacked him for not supporting his wife, and Mrs Jones criticized her father for not supporting her mother. Grandfather retaliated by blaming his wife for neglecting all her children – in short, a Pandora's Box seemed to have been opened. There was clearly a lot of unfinished business – to do with who was a good parent and who was a bad one. Further sessions were offered and the same foursome attended on two further occasions.*

One of the major tasks of family therapy is to help people deal with unfinished business. As these issues are usually too hot for families to handle on their own, they never get discussed at home because people get steamed up and slam doors or walk out. In a therapy session family members are more likely to stay in the room. This enables them to listen to what cannot usually be listened to and say what cannot usually be said. Family therapists will help the individuals look at patterns that have been passed from generation to generation, old scripts and redundant myths. Drawing up a family tree and other techniques described elsewhere in this book will help the family members make these connections. In successive family sessions everyone gets closer to the core of the 'onion' – and on the way some practical issues are addressed.

*During the next two sessions issues from Mrs Jones's childhood were brought up, her parents' apprehensions about her choosing Mr Jones as her partner, and what happened when she moved back to live with her parents for the two years after Emily's birth. The family recognized that Mrs Jones and her mother had been competing as to who could be the 'better' mother and that Emily had been very much caught up in this. Grandmother acknowledged that she had tried to spoil Emily and Mother said she had reacted against this by being more strict. Gradually they all came to see how much both Mother's and Grandmother's responses were linked.*

*The family then started to think how to make life easier for Emily so that she would not become too confused by the different*

*inputs from her parents and grandparents. A fairly detailed
plan was worked out, particularly involving who Emily should
listen to and who had the final say – Mother or Grandmother.
With the help of the therapist the adults looked at a number of
hypothetical situations that were likely to occur and what each
family member might do or say to avoid confusing Emily.*

In family therapy there is a continuous shift to and from
focusing on complex trans-generational issues and concentrating on apparently trivial everyday issues. There is no contradiction in this: unresolved issues from the past are reflected in
daily kitchen-sink problems, so focusing on the latter deals
with the former and vice versa. How people negotiate over who
does the washing up or carries the rubbish out is related to
their earlier experiences of division of labour, gender roles,
decision-making etc. If these connect with problematic issues
in the past they can cause difficulties in the present.

*A fortnight later Emily, her brother and sister, the parents and
the grandparents all attended the session together. It was a
lively family meeting and it was very impressive to see how they
all worked together. The parents were clearly in charge of the
children, and when the children turned to their grandparents,
in an effort to involve them and contradict the parents'
instructions, the grandparents handed responsibility back to the
parents. Everyone acknowledged that there had been
considerable changes and the parents confirmed that they now
had no difficulties handling the children in their own home.
They added, however, that Emily still played up whenever they
were all at the grandparents' house.*

*After some negotiation it was agreed that the next session
would take place in the grandparents' home – with everyone
present. This was arranged for the following week. The therapist
was greeted by Emily who asked whether he wanted to see her
mother's old room – Emily had taken it over. The grandparents
agreed and she led the expedition to the top floor. Everyone
squeezed into the smallish room. Emily proudly pointed out her
mother's old toys which had now become hers. Suddenly Emily's
mother burst into tears and wept uncontrollably . . .*

Seeing families in their homes is something that many family therapists will consider. It is up to the family to evaluate whether this would be useful or would constitute an unwanted intrusion. Quite a few families feel that the problems happen at home and discussing them in a consulting room in a clinic is too far removed from their daily reality. Moreover, parents might say 'We can do this here . . . but we couldn't do it at home – because the telephone never stops ringing, our house is too big/too small', and so on. How people arrange their living spaces often both reflects and contributes to the problems they are experiencing. Trying new things out in familiar spaces is often a necessary step which may require the presence of the therapist.

> *Only Emily's parents came to the next session. They reported that as far as the children were concerned things were fine. They now felt the need to discuss some issues affecting their own relationship and did not think it right to have Mrs Jones's parents in on that. Mrs Jones said it had all suddenly 'come together' and that her crying in her old bedroom had sparked off some very good talks with her husband.*
>
> *In the session both Mr and Mrs Jones talked about how all these years she had felt torn between her parents and her husband. She had started living with him in order to get away from them, having always felt the least loved of their three children. Her very mixed feelings had come to the surface after Emily's birth and this led to her reconnecting with her parents. Through Emily, she then indirectly received some of the parenting that she felt was withheld from her when she was a small child.*
>
> *When she returned to live with Emily's father she found it very difficult to leave her parents' house and this is why, without being aware of it, she 'planted' Emily there. Having Emily live with her grandparents part-time kept the issue alive. Mrs Jones saw her grandmother 'making good' through her grandchild which evoked mixed feelings in her. She felt pleased for Emily but also envious: why had her mother not been able to do for her what she was obviously capable of doing for Emily?*
>
> *Both Mr and Mrs Jones then looked at how this arrangement*

*may have suited them both. The focus now shifted on to Mr
Jones and how this gave him the space he felt he needed, being
very young at the time of Emily's birth. It had enabled him to
keep up contact with his parents and pursue his own career, but
in the process it had stopped them becoming a family. The
couple asked for one more session to discuss a way forward for
them, both as a family and as a married couple.*

*A year later the family wrote to the therapist, saying that their
children were thriving, that all three children went to stay with
the grandparents once a month for the weekend, and that they
were a 'normal family' now.*

Family therapy does not set out to 'cure' people. Instead it aims
to set a process in motion, like jump-starting an engine and
making sure it turns over on its own before removing the jump-
leads. Which direction the engine, or rather the family, wants
to move in afterwards is up to them. The therapist can take the
family on a guided tour of new possible scenarios but only the
family can decide which of them they subsequently want to
inhabit.

### How long does family therapy take?
The Jones family had another two sessions (parents only),
making it ten in all. The first few sessions are often close
together, perhaps weekly, and then they are spaced out at
fortnightly or monthly intervals. On average, families go for
between six and twelve therapy sessions. Many families improve, others don't.

Why does family therapy not go on forever? Family therapists
try to avoid creating dependencies and, since the family becomes the 'co-therapist' during the course of therapy, things
can carry on after the therapist has left, having prepared the
family to continue the work started in the 'official' therapy
sessions. When family members become too dependent on the
therapist, they may – sometimes without realizing – create new
problems in order to continue receiving therapy.

## THE DANGERS AND BENEFITS OF FAMILY THERAPY

Like a packet of cigarettes, any therapy should carry a health warning. Therapy aims to promote change, and change can be very unsettling. Being stuck in a malignant alliance, for example, may be unpleasant but at least it's familiar. The alternative may be better but is unknown. Change is a slow process, not only because many of us seem to be married to our problems but also because of the fear of the unknown. Change means taking risks.

Family therapists do not set out to mend families – or to rip them apart for that matter. They try to provide a setting where both the implications of continuing the same way and of changing familiar routines can be constructively discussed. The therapist cannot and should not decide what people do with their lives. Family therapy, however, does offer choices and asks the family and its members to weigh up the pros and cons of staying together or living apart. If increasing choices is subversive then family therapy is subversive.

At one time family therapy may have been a bag of tricks unleashed on to unsuspecting families. But the modern family therapist is – hopefully – not a whizz-kid technician. Instead he or she is a human being with good professional skills. Family therapy has come of age – there is less mystery and more transparency.

There is now plenty of evidence that family therapy has a valuable contribution to make, not only when it comes to solving people's immediate relationship problems but also in treating serious forms of psychological disturbance. These may include eating disorders, behavioural problems, depression, schizophrenia, emotional problems in children, and adolescent breakdown.

Family therapy has its limitations and at times it may be appropriate for one or more members to get some individual help afterwards. It is not a panacea for everything and everyone. But it's certainly worth trying when the family can no longer help itself.

# Useful Addresses

## Adoption

**BAAF** (*BRITISH AGENCIES FOR ADOPTION AND FOSTERING*)
11 Southwark Street
London SE1 1RQ
Tel: 0171 407 8800

**NORCAP** (*NATIONAL ORGANISATION FOR COUNSELLING ADOPTEES AND THEIR PARENTS*)
3 New High Street
Headington
Oxford OX3 7AJ
Helpline: 01865 750554

**POST-ADOPTION CENTRE**
8 Torriano Mews
Torriano Avenue
London NW5 2RZ
Tel: 0171 284 0555

## Ageing

**COUNSEL AND CARE**
Twyman House
16 Bonny Street
London NW1 9PG
Tel: 0171 485 1566

**HELP THE AGED**
St James's Walk
London EC1R 0BE
Helpline: 0800 289404

## Alcohol and Addiction Problems

**AL-ANON** FAMILY GROUPS
61 Great Dover Street
London SE1 4YS
Helpline: 0171 403 0888

**DRINKLINE**
13–14 West Smithfield
London EC1A 9DH
Tel: 0171 332 0150
Helpline: 0171 332 0202

**FAMILIES ANONYMOUS**
Unit 37
Charlotte Despard Avenue
London SW11 5JE
Tel: 0171 498 4680

**RELEASE**
388 Old Street
London EC1V 9LT
Helplines: 0171 729 9904
0171 603 8654

## Bereavement

**THE COMPASSIONATE FRIENDS**
53 North Street
Bristol BS3 1EN
Tel: 01179 665202
Helpline: 01272 539639

**CRUSE**
Cruse House
126 Sheen Road
Richmond Surrey TW9 1UR
Tel: 0181 940 4818
Helpline: 0181 332 7227

**NATIONAL ASSOCIATION OF BEREAVEMENT SERVICES**
20 Norton Folgate
London E1 6DB
Tel: 0171 247 1080

## Child Abuse and Neglect

**CHILDLINE**
2nd Floor
Royal Mail Building
Studd Street
London N1 0QW
Helpline: 0800 1111

**NSPCC**
67 Saffron Hill
London EC1N 8RS
Helpline: 0800 800500

**NEWPIN**
Sutherland House
London SE17 3EE
Tel: 0171 703 6326

## Disabilities

**CONTACT-A-FAMILY**
16 Strutton Ground
London SW1P 2HP
Helpline: 0171 222 2695

**CROSSROADS**
10 Regent Place
Rugby
Warwickshire CV21 2PN
Tel: 01788 573653

**MENCAP**
123 Golden Lane
London EC1Y 0RT
Tel: 0171 454 0454

## Eating Disorders

**EATING DISORDERS ASSOCIATION**
Sackville Place
44 Magdalen Street
Norwich
Norfolk NR3 1JU
Helpline: 01603 621414

## Family Planning

**FAMILY PLANNING ASSOCIATION**
27–35 Mortimer Street
London W1N 7RJ
Tel: 0171 636 7866

**LIFE**
1A Newbold Terrace
Leamington Spa
Warwickshire CV32 4EA
Helpline: 01926 311511

**NATIONAL CHILDBIRTH TRUST**
Alexandra House
Oldham Terrace
London W3 6NH
Tel: 0181 992 8637

## Family Therapy

Family therapy is available within
many public sector services, such as
child and adult psychiatry, social
services, general practice and other
settings. In addition there are
many family therapists who work
privately. However it can be quite
difficult to be referred to the
appropriate professional and you
may have to rely on your GP or
personal recommendations. The
AFT (Association for Family
Therapy) has a nationwide list of
family therapists:

**AFT (*ASSOCIATION FOR FAMILY THERAPY*)**
18 Winnipeg Drive
Lakeside
Cardiff CF2 6ET
Tel: 01222 753162

The following institutions, some of
which are NHS clinics or charities,
provide family therapy as part of
their services:

**BARNARDOS FAMILY THERAPY SERVICE**
Mornington Terrace
29 Upper Duke Street
Liverpool L1 9DY
Tel: 0151 709 0540

FAMILY INSTITUTE
105 Cathedral Road
Cardiff CF1 9PH
Tel: 01222 226532

INSTITUTE OF FAMILY THERAPY
43 New Cavendish Street
London W1M 7RG
Tel: 0171 935 1651

KENSINGTON CONSULTATION CENTRE
47 South Lambeth Road
London SW8 1RH
Tel: 0171 793 0148

MARLBOROUGH FAMILY SERVICE
38 Marlborough Place
London NW8 0PJ
Tel: 0171 624 8605

MAUDSLEY HOSPITAL
Psychotherapy Department
Denmark Hill
London SE5 8AZ
Tel: 0171 919 2385

SCOTTISH INSTITUTE OF HUMAN RELATIONS
56 Albany Street
Edinburgh EH1 3QR
Tel: 0131 556 0924

TAVISTOCK CLINIC
120 Belsize Lane
London NW3 5BA
Tel: 0171 435 7111

WESTMINSTER PASTORAL FOUNDATION
23 Kensington Square
London W8 5HN
Tel: 0171 937 6956

YORK HOUSE FAMILY CLINIC
York House
Manchester Royal Infirmary
Oxford Road
Manchester M13 9BX
Tel: 0161 2765313

## Marriage and Separation

DOMESTIC VIOLENCE INTERVENTION PROJECT
PO Box 2838
London W6 9ZE
Violence Prevention Programme for Men
Tel: 0181 563 7983
Women's Support Service
Tel: 0181 748 6512

NATIONAL FAMILY CONCILIATION COUNCIL
Shaftesbury Centre
Percy Street
Swindon
Wiltshire SN2 2AZ
Tel: 01793 514055

ONE PLUS ONE
12 New Burlington Street
London W1X 1FF
Tel: 0171 734 2020

REFUGE
Tel: 0181 747 0133
Crisisline: 0181 995 4430

RELATE
Herbert Gray College
Little Church Street
Rugby
Warwickshire CV21 3AP
Tel: 01788 573241

## Mental Illness

**ASSOCIATION FOR POST-NATAL ILLNESS**
25 Jerdan Place
London SW6 1BE
Helpline: 0171 386 0868

**MIND**
Granta House
15–19 Broadway
London E15 4BQ
Tel: 0181 519 2122
0181 522 1725

**SANELINE**
199–205 Old Marylebone Road
London NW1 5QP
Helpline: 0171 724 8000

## Parenthood

**EXPLORING PARENTHOOD**
Latimer Education Centre
194 Freston Road
London W10 6TT
Tel: 0181 960 1678

**FAMILIES NEED FATHERS**
134 Curtain Road
London EC2A 3AR
Tel: 0171 613 5060
Helpline: 0181 886 0970

**FFLAG** – *FAMILIES AND FRIENDS OF LESBIANS AND GAYS*
PO Box 153
Manchester M60 1LP
Helplines: 0161 628 7621
01162 708331

**HOME START UK**
2 Salisbury Road
Leicester LE7 7QR
Tel: 01162 554988

**MAMA** (*MEET-A-MUM ASSOCIATION*)
14 Illis Road
Croydon CR0 2XX
Helpline: 0181 656 7318

**PARENTLINE**
Westbury House
57 Hart Road
Thundersley
Essex SS7 3PP
Helpline: 01268 757077

**WORKING MOTHERS/PARENTS AT WORK**
77 Holloway Road
London N7 8JZ
Helpline: 0171 700 5771

## Single Parents

**GINGERBREAD**
35 Wellington Street
London WC2E 7BN
Advicelines: 0171 240 0953
0141 353 0953
01232 234568
01792 648728

## Step-Families

**STEPFAMILY** (*NATIONAL STEPFAMILY ASSOCIATION*)
72 Willesden Lane
London NW6 7TA
Tel: 0171 372 0844
Helpline: 0171 372 0846

# Further Reading

**General Books on Family Therapy**
Bruggen, P. & O'Brian, C., *Surviving Adolescence*, Faber and Faber, 1986
Laing, R.D. & Esterson, A., *Sanity, Madness and the Family*, Basic Books, 1971
Napier, A. & Whitaker, C., *The Family Crucible*, Harper and Row, 1978
Skynner, R. & Cleese, J., *Families and How to Survive Them*, Methuen, 1983; Mandarin, 1993
Watzlawick, P., Weakland, J. & Fish, R., *Change: Principles of Problem Formation and Problem Resolution*, W. W. Norton, 1974

**Family Therapy Classics**
Ackerman, N.W., *Treating the Troubled Family*, Basic Books, 1967
Haley, J., *Problem-solving Therapy*, Jossey-Bass, 1977
Hoffman, L., *Foundations of Family Therapy*, Basic Books, 1981
Minuchin, S., *Families and Family Therapy*, Tavistock, 1974
Satir, V., *Peoplemaking*, Souvenir Press, 1972
Selvini Palazzoli, M., Boscolo, L., Cecchin, L. & Prata, G., *Paradox and Counterparadox*, J. Aronson, 1978
Watzlawick, P., Jackson, D. & Beavin, J., *Pragmatics of Human Communication*, W. W. Norton, 1967

**Recent Family Therapy Books**
Boyd-Franklin, N., *Black Families in Therapy: A Multisystems Approach*, Guildford Press, 1989
Burnham, J., *Family Therapy*, Tavistock, 1986
Carpenter, J. & Treacher, A. (eds.), *Using Family Therapy in the 90s*, Blackwell, 1994
Carter, E. & McGoldrick, M., *The Changing Family Life Cycle: A Framework for Family Therapy*, 2nd edition, Allyn & Bacon, 1989
Jones, E., *Family Systems Therapy*, John Wiley & Sons, 1993
Robinson, M., *Family Transformation Through Divorce and Remarriage: A Systemic Approach*, Routledge, 1991

# Index